Spinderella

He Turned IT

Revised Edition

By Angie L. Keaton Wiggins

A Faith Investment from _____ to promote your turn of events.

From my Heart,

*_____,
to Yours.*

Copyright© 2021
by Angie L. Keaton Wiggins
ISBN: 978-0-9786898-0-3

All rights reserved. No part of this publication may be reproduced, stored in a retrieval system, or transmitted in any form or by any means, electronic, mechanical, photocopying, recording or otherwise, without prior written permission of the publisher.

Book Cover
Illustration: Angie L. Keaton Wiggins
                 Auguiste George &
                 Vector Design by Shutterstock
Hair Stylist: Styles by Salesia
Photographer: Erick Robinson Photography
Scripture: New King James Version®
                 unless otherwise noted.
1st Edition: Copyright© 2019
Revised Ed.:   Copyright© 2021

Printed in the United States of America.

ALK Coaching & Productions
coaching@alkcopro.com

Table of Contents

Preface:		12
Introduction:		13

Part I: A PERSON

Chapter 1:	Tag, You're IT - Not a Game for the Faint-hearted	19
Chapter 2:	Deal with IT - or IT will Deal with You	33

Part II: A PROBLEM

Chapter 3:	You've Got Me Going in Circles	53
Chapter 4:	New Outlook + New Approach = Change	67

Part III: THE PROBLEM SOLVER

Chapter 5:	Power of Agreement - The LORD Takes Notice	85
Chapter 6:	He Turned IT - Shut Up & Open Up	93
Chapter 7:	*Spinderella's* Prayer of Thanksgvg.	103
Chapter 8:	Testimonials	107

Dedication

This Book is in Gratitude to -
My Heavenly Father, Savior and Holy Spirit
That I may publish with the voice of thanksgiving
and tell of all thy wondrous works. - Psalm 26:7

In Memory of two Phenomenal Women -
My Grandmother, Annie "Ms. AV" Johnson Plummer
My Friend from High School - JCHS Class of 1984 -
Palestine "Pal" Mays Atkins

In Salute to -
My Beloved Parents, Abraham & Josephine Keaton

Children & Grandchild
Brandon Wiggins / April & Hailey (GiGi Baby)
Holmes / Robert Austin Wiggins

God-Children
Vershauna Mays-Banks / Michael Dwayne Atkins /
Marquasha Keaton / Dexter William Martin /
Lydia Nichole Brooks

Siblings
Gary Robinson / Melva (Wayne) Saunders /
Terry (Lori) Keaton / Tonnette Cassandra Keaton /
Cheryl (Detroit) Griffin

Lovingly,
Ann

Endorsements

"To God be the glory! The Woman of God has now birthed the book prophesied to her years ago. It is sure to be a great blessing."

                               - Dr. L. E. Cohen, III, Pastor
                         In His Presence Cathedral of Praise

"Encouraging, refreshing, emerging prophetic powerhouse is how I describe Angie Wiggins. This book will cause a divine shift in the mind of the reader which will produce a major breakthrough in the lives of people for generations to come. Prepare to enjoy *'Spinderella'* as you flow through each chapter that reflects on real stories of tests, trials, teachings and triumphant victories. If The LORD turned IT for Angie and *Spinderella*, He can Turn IT for you!"

                             - Dr. Nicky E. Collins, Pastor
                       Higher Dimension Church Tallahassee

"This book is a must-read, brilliantly done!"
                         - Chad Lawson & Alicia Robinson Cooper

"Prophetess Angie Wiggins is providing an inspirational and critical message to readers in this book which is based on our need to 'trust God and lean not to our own understanding.' Real life examples document that God has a plan for our lives and His plan is ALWAYS the best plan. Kudos to Angie on her most recent endeavor in printed word to share the Word of God with the people of God."

                     - Anita R. Favors, Retired City Manager

"People are faced with problems and situations that they do not have the ways and means to solve them. However, *Spinderella* introduces us to the real Problem Solver. It is a well thought out practical book steeped in scriptures that offers hope to everyone... no matter the race, religion, cultural background, no matter what IT is, The LORD can turn IT around. There is nothing too hard for Him! It is a great tool which displays the evidence of The LORD's providence for His people. Many shall be changed by reading *Spinderella*."

— Deshone D. Hedrington, Executive Pastor
The Father's House Unlimited Ministries

"Prophetess Angie Keaton Wiggins is truly a vessel of The LORD! She is dedicated, passionate, and determined to fulfill His pre-ordained destiny for her life. She has been chosen, called, and appointed to write, preach, and prophesy! I love it that she shares that 'The LORD gives us a birth date and a mandate to fulfill in the earth;' however, when you are anointed at times you will be disappointed. This is why as an individual that has seen The LORD turn things around for my good, I say that this is a must-read book for anyone that has or is facing life challenges. She walks us through a difficult time in her life and also takes us on a journey perusing the frustrations Hannah endured in her life. Let this be your source of inspiration as she guides you through the Turn Around process. I can truly say that in life I have been Tagged for a Turn Around and you never know you may be next... 'tag, you're It!'"

— Jeanette Lindsey, Founder and President
Kingdom Living Ministry Tallahassee, Inc.

"Prophetess Angie Wiggins's *Spinderella:* He Turned IT is informative, educational and inspiring. It provides wisdom and insight on how to effectively grow through a process when becoming what God said. *Spinderella,* like so many others, learns that Peninnah is necessary for your process. Harassing spirits provoke until we cry out to God. He then raises up a deliverer. The wisdom keys provided in this book along with lessons learned will impact your life positively and like *Spinderella,* birth the will of God. I highly recommend this book."

- Apostle Lee A. Lyons
Priestly Praise Ministries, Inc.

"*Spinderella:* He Turned IT is a blast of inspiration! Applause Angie for weaving scriptures into life's scenarios to remind us that through our trials we can hold fast to an expectation of triumph because our God is true to His Word. Your use of real-life testimonials further reinforces the awesome omnipotence of the Author and Finisher of our faith in our daily lives! Well done, Prophetess Angie!"

- Carmen Cummings Martin

"*Spinderella* is a lite-changing empowerment asset that pushes and coaches every reader to SHIFT while personifying victory to the glory of God. The process to change includes a willing person that is bold enough to admit there is a problem by faith to The Problem Solver. Many people that read this book will turn around and sow a seed into this superb author because the deposit is too rich not to do so."

- Dr. YaQuanda McCall, Senior Leader @ 5AM Prayer SHIFTers
CEO/Founder, I Speak Life Global Ministries, Inc.

"We have had the opportunity to observe Angie Wiggins's ministry up close and personal for many years. What is clear is Angie is indeed a true Woman of God. *Spinderella* provides compelling insight to the reader. This book will encourage the reader that all is not lost when circumstances happen, keep the faith and continue the course; God is indeed faithful."

- Apostle Alzo & Dr. Teresa Slade
Potter's House Ministries

"I am honored to be selected as one of the ones to endorse Prophetess Angie Wiggins' new book, '*Spinderella*: He Turned IT.' I have known Angie as a personal friend for over 20 years, and I have viewed her character on and off the job, and I have witnessed her loyalty to friendship, ministry, and leadership. While serving multiple leaders and yet remaining humble, she has always prioritized and has been #1 while being #2. Well, I believe that this is her harvest season, where she will lead with joy. I am so excited that she has chosen to begin by authoring this mind-blowing, educational tool called book.

Prophetess Wiggins will share with you, that while praying together, I stated to her, during one of her toughest moments, 'to make God look good.' Because she decided to Grow through, while she Go through, I believe that this book is a vault of experiences, that will bring new light, in dark places to many people, who choose to open their hearts to keys that can unlock the power of agreement and stop going in the circles of life. She declares, 'You can no longer hide in the crowd as a 'tag along,' nor go along to get along.' As The LORD's prophetic mouthpiece, I proclaim to you today, if you did not know it before, you surely do now- -- 'tag, you're It!'

Open your hearts and minds to receive this hand-crafted work, from such an anointed vessel who has the heart of The LORD. This book will transform lives and helps heal hidden areas of hurt and abuse. I pray this book help you understand that He has already turned IT for you, so as Prophetess Wiggins instructs us, tag and bless another person and say BAM! you're it, and already blessed."

- Dr. Delaine Smith

"I stand in awe of this extraordinary book. *Spinderella* will certainly inspire and challenge readers to boldly pursue their dreams with confidence, courage, and great expectation. The book is a shining light of hope for all!"

- Dr. Marilyn Todman, CEO and Founder
Preach The Word Network TV

"*Spinderella* is a must read. The prophetic insight and revelatory knowledge presented caused my spirit man to leap and the intercessor in me to arise like never before. *Spinderella* also ignited the flames of fire in my faith with hope to keep trusting God in the process. It caused me to have a fresh new perspective on life regardless of past challenges. Prophet Angie Wiggins, a.k.a. "Ann," you are a blessing in my life and to the Kingdom. I'm grateful to God that **He Turned IT!**"

- Apostle Otis B. Young, Ph.D.
Senior Pastor, Kingdom Life Tabernacle
CEO, Kingdom Life Preparatory Academy

Preface

The Battle of Shiloh fought April 6-7, 1862, in southwestern Tennessee is known as one of the most important battles of the American Civil War. The overpowering Confederate offensive drove the unprepared Federal forces from their camps and threatened to overwhelm Ulysses S. Grant's entire command. Grant's April 7th counteroffensive overpowered the weakened Confederate forces and Beauregard's army retired from the field. [1]

While the *Battle of Shiloh* in this great USA ended with casualties and bloodshed, a civilian war and battlefield of the mind commenced centuries earlier at another historic Shiloh. *The turn of events was epic. The adversary never saw IT coming.*

---

[1] Wikipedia contributors. "Battle of Shiloh." *Wikipedia, The Free Encyclopedia*. Wikipedia, The Free Encyclopedia, 8 Jan. 2019. Web. 9 Jan. 2019.

Introduction

*"It's been a long, a long time coming
But I know a change gonna come, Oh, yes it will..."
A Change Is Gonna Come
- the late great Sam Cooke*

Happy New Year, or is it?

Anticipation is building. Will this be the year to cheer for answered prayer? It started and was about to end as numerous others that had come and gone. Then, IT happened...

Every year like clockwork, Hannah, her family, and community, make the long journey to the holy place, Shiloh. It means tranquility but seldom is she privy to peaceful worship and fellowship. All Hannah is accustomed to are two annoyances: A shut-up womb that The LORD read the Miranda rights to remain silent. And, years of tears and silent frustration provoked by the other wife. Judged and misjudged due to the unfavorable condition that The LORD put her in, Hannah's life is constantly *revolving* in circles, yet never evolving forward.

All of that is about to change! If you like, "Cinderella," the story of a girl who endured a process of adverse conditions, but she overcame those challenges, you will love, *Spinderella: He Turned IT.* Founded on the chronicles of Hannah (a.k.a. *"Spinderella"*) according to the Biblical Book of 1 Samuel.

Hannah caught my attention with some productive shifts and turns that she made. That is why I renamed her, *Spinderella*. Her biblical name means favor, grace and full of prayer. Read and witness the impact of her favor on her adversary, the power of her prayer, and an uncalculated risk that she took. The move gained a priest's attention and garnered The LORD's intervention. Afterward, she partnered with Him and produced what they both desired.

I first became interested in the life of *Spinderella* 12+ years ago. The LORD used me to preach about her in a sermon. The title was, *PUSH, POP, Don't Stop until the Baby DROP!* Congregants were enlightened and encouraged by the message to Pray Until Something Happens (PUSH) because the Power Of Prayer (POP) causes things to DROP (Desires Reaped Over Prayer). A few years later, I encountered a major life-changing event. Like *Spinderella,* IT had my life *revolving* in circles, yet never evolving forward. I was reminded of the message. The second time around, the sermon was lived out for five years in the public's eyes versus talked out from behind a podium.

To my surprise, the chronicles of Hannah *"Spinderella"* reminded me of my life - A Person, with A Problem, in need of The Problem Solver. My name is Angie, a.k.a "Ann." Ann is in the name Hannah. She was barren and sought The LORD to be able to deliver. My finances were drastically impacted, and I sought him for deliverance. I delved deeper into the life of *Spinderella,* and I realized that we have deep similarities. Her story is also about A Person, with A Problem, in need of The Problem Solver. This book revolves around three significant parts:

A Person: The Prophet Jeremiah (Jeremiah 1:5) proclaimed that The LORD knows A Person's birth date and mandate. When the fullness of time comes, it is then that A Person is *"tagged it,"* and begins life in the earth.

A Problem: An adversary or adverse situation. It does not matter A Person's age, race or social status, at a point reached in life, every Person will encounter A Problem. Google.com defines A Problem as, "a matter or situation regarded as unwelcome or harmful and needing to be dealt with and overcome; a thing that is difficult to achieve or accomplish." Everyone has a fiscal, physical, or psychological problem to overcome.

The Problem Solver: You can remain confident that when faced with an unfavorable condition, The LORD, The Problem Solver, is on high alert to offer prevention or intervention. A "problem solver is a thinker who focuses on the problem as stated and tries to synthesize information and knowledge to achieve a solution..." [2]

---

[2] "problem solver." WordNet 3.0, Farlex clipart collection. 2003-2008. Princeton University, Clipart.com, Farlex Inc. 8 Jan. 2019 https://www.thefreedictionary.com/problem+solver

Some of you have tolerated a problem so long that IT revolved into a condition. You are not your condition. That is subject to change. What happened to you does not define you. IT refines you. Be encouraged that help is on the way if you do not give up or out during your series of actions that lead to your expected end.

This book is 12+ years in the making. As I developed over the years, so did the title and content. It is a compelling, life-changing process that proves that The LORD can turn your IT around for your good. It reveals that you, too, can become an active player in your process toward success.

Spinderella: He Turned IT, offers hope to a wide audience. It includes thought-provoking "Pivotal Moments," arranged throughout the book that led to productive turning points. Also included are testimonies from couples who received a turnaround in their faith and families.

This publication is more than just another good book. It is designed to revolutionize the way that you view and respond to your IT. Isn't it time for your desire to turn into your reality?

Like me, your IT may not be the same as *Spinderella's*. The reward from reading this book is that you can benefit from the process that she experienced. The LORD is not a respecter of persons. He is a respecter of His principles - faith and patience. When faith and patience meet opportunity, change occurs. If you incorporate His principles into your affairs, you, too, will go down in history with the same testimony as *Spinderella - He Turned IT!*

-A Person-

...A being that has certain capacities or attributes such as reason, morality, consciousness or self-consciousness... [3]

The Affect
Touch the feelings of; move emotionally; influence behavior. [4]

---

[3] Wikipedia contributors. "Person." *Wikipedia, The Free Encyclopedia*. Wikipedia, The Free Encyclopedia, 31 Dec. 2018. Web. 9 Jan. 2019.

[4] "Affect | Definition of Affect in English by Oxford Dictionaries." *Oxford Dictionaries | English*, Oxford Dictionaries, en.oxforddictionaries.com/definition/affect.

CHAPTER 1

Tag, You're IT

For if you remain completely silent at this time, relief and deliverance will arise for the Jews from another place, but you and your father's house will perish. Yet who knows whether you have come to the kingdom for such a time as this? - Esther 4:14

When I was a child a popular game to play was "Tag, You're IT." The activity involved two or more players and a leader who selected which player became IT first. The competitor identified as IT chased additional players, touched one of them, then publicly announced, "tag, you're IT." When the new IT stepped into position, the game moved forward, and the player who tagged that person moved off the scene.

A similar scenario occurs in this game of life. The difference is that The LORD is Leader and Tagger. He knows the end from the beginning and has fashioned our lives according to our purpose in the earth. He looked at what He had made, and behold, it was good. The LORD assigned to every person a birth and death date and a mandate to fulfill in the earth. It is He who assigns skin color, nationality, and genealogy. Afterward, A Person is sent to earth to aid in The LORD's redemptive plan for man. All humans are *fearfully and wonderfully made (Psalm 139:14).* A Designer's original who should not die a carbon copy of someone other than Him, nor die before the mandate is fulfilled (Ecclesiastes 7:17; Psalm 55:23).

Every human born of a woman - the doors of life into the earth - have a part to play. If not, *Spinderella,* you and I would not have been born. Yes, you are included and not excluded. You are either following in the footsteps of someone that came before you or blazing a new path that others will follow when the time of your departure is at hand.

When the fullness of time comes for A Person to shift off the scene, the successor has already been identified and tagged, "you're IT."

> *But when the fullness of the time had come, God sent forth His Son, born of a woman, born under the law...*
> *- Galatians 4:4*
>
> *And so it was, when they had crossed over, that Elijah said to Elisha, "Ask! What may I do for you, before I am taken away from you?" Elisha said, "Please let a double portion of your spirit be upon me." So he said, "You have asked a hard thing. Nevertheless, if you see me when I am taken from you, it shall be so for you; but if not, it shall not be so." Then it happened, as they continued on and talked, that suddenly a chariot of fire appeared with horses of*

> *fire and separated the two of them; and Elijah went up by a whirlwind into heaven. And Elisha saw it, and he cried out, "My father, my father, the chariot of Israel and its horsemen!" So he saw him no more. And he took hold of his own clothes and tore them into pieces. Then he took the mantle of Elijah that had fallen from him, and struck the water, and said, "Where is the Lord God of Elijah?" And when he also had struck the water, it was divided this way and that; and Elisha crossed over. Now when the sons of the prophets who were from Jericho saw him, they said, "The spirit of Elijah rests on Elisha." And they came to meet him, and bowed to the ground before him.*
> *- II Kings 2:9-12, 14-15*

The Prophet Elijah could not take his mantle (cloak; an important role or responsibility that passes from one person to another) [5] with him to Heaven when he departed the earth-realm. Why? It was a *man*-tle; not operable nor needed in Heaven.

---

[5] "Mantle | Definition of Mantle in English by Oxford Dictionaries." *Oxford Dictionaries | English*, Oxford Dictionaries, en.oxforddictionaries.com/definition/mantle.

Specialists at Work

Since the creation of time, there have been "specialists" who were tagged IT. Some earthly assignments affect a small group of people. Specialists are endowed with unique purposes and skills that impact generations, nations and the world.

> *Before I formed you in the womb I knew you; Before you were born I sanctified you; I ordained you a prophet to the nations.* - Jeremiah 1:5

The next level playing field that they are called to can cost them their families, reputations, will-power, and lives. This dimension of the game of life is not for the faint-hearted.

Take *Noah* for example. In his era, the earthly inhabitants had grown corrupt and violent. He was tagged IT to build an ark to be saved from a flood that would rid the world of violence and unrighteousness. The people of his day saw him as a crazy, old, drunk man who spoke of a substance - rain - that they had never seen. Not until it was too late. Noah and his family were preserved. The LORD established a covenant with them and every living creature (Genesis Chapters 6-9).

Abraham begat Isaac. Isaac begat Jacob. Abraham, the patriarch of the family, was the first to be tagged IT. He became the father of many nations and the father of faith. Before the fulfillment of his assignment on earth, his son, Isaac, had already shifted into position as the next IT. The LORD repeated to Isaac the Abrahamic Covenant (Genesis 12:1-3). He continued in the work that his father started. Afterward, the spotlight shifted off Isaac and onto his son, *Jacob*.

He was *created* as Jacob (the natural man; trickster was in his bloodline). The LORD used his past to build his future; therefore, He *formed* Israel (the spiritual man) from Jacob. The LORD formed him into what He needed him to be.

> *But now, thus says the LORD, who created you, O Jacob, and He who formed you, O Israel...*
> *- Isaiah 43:1*

> *And the vessel that he made of clay was marred in the hand of the potter; so, he made it again into another vessel, as it seemed good to the potter to make.*
> *- Jeremiah 18:4*

Joseph was tagged IT to preserve the lives of his family and homeland. He became a father to Pharaoh and a ruler throughout all the land of Egypt (Genesis 45). Prior to seeing his dream become a reality, it placed him on trial. He was tested in a pit and prison, but resurrected and perfected for his next dimension of leading and living---in a palace.

> *Until the time that his word came to pass, the word of the LORD tested him.*
> *- Psalm 105:19*

> *But now, do not therefore be grieved or angry with yourselves because you sold me here; for God sent me before you to preserve life. And God sent me before you to preserve a posterity for you in the earth, and to save your lives by a great deliverance. So now it was not you who sent me here, but God...*
> *- Genesis 45:5, 7-8*

Moses was tagged IT. He had to grow into his role of the deliverer. Moses complained that he was not an eloquent speaker, but he stepped out in faith. He committed murder. He ran in fear for his life, but boldly fulfilled his assignment to bring The LORD's people out of Egypt. Moses allowed the people's murmuring and complaining to cause him to disobey The LORD's instructions. He was allowed to see the promised land, but not to enter that which was promised (ref. Numbers 20:7-12).

Joshua, Moses' minister, was tagged IT as his successor. Moses led the people out of Egypt. Joshua led them into the promised land. Moses lifted his rod over the Red Sea, and it separated. Joshua and the priests carrying the ark of the covenant stepped into the waters of Jordan and it separated.

> *Moses My servant is dead. Now therefore, arise, go over this Jordan, you and all this people, to the land which I am giving to them - the children of Israel. Every place that the sole of your foot will tread upon I have given you, as I said to Moses.*
> *- Joshua 1:2-3*

> *And the LORD said to Joshua, "This day I will begin to exalt you in the sight of all Israel, that they may know that, as I was with Moses, so I will be with you.*
> *-Joshua 3:7*

Spinderella petitioned The LORD for a male child. Unknown to her, she was tagged IT because of the vacant position for a loyal priest. In the end, she and The LORD's teamwork made their desires work.

> *Then she made a vow and said, "O LORD of hosts, if You will indeed look on the affliction of Your maidservant and remember me, and not forget Your maidservant, but wilt give Your maidservant a male child, then I will give him to the LORD all the days of his life, and no razor shall come upon his head."   - 1 Samuel 1:11*

> *Then I will raise up for Myself a faithful priest who shall do according to what is in My heart and in My mind. I will build him a sure house: and he shall walk before My anointed forever.*
>
> *- 1 Samuel 2:35*

You just witnessed examples of "specialists" whom The LORD tagged, IT.

You are the IT of your family, ministry, community, state and world. Life's journey sometimes becomes more than you can bear. You will desire to be tagged out of the game and shutdown on your assignment just as the Prophet Jeremiah did. He was sent to the earth by The LORD as a <u>pre</u>-ordained prophet. When times grew weary, he declared that he would not speak again in The LORD's name. His declaration changed when the heat was on, from the inside out!

> *O LORD, You induced me, and I was persuaded; You are stronger than I, and have prevailed. I am in derision daily; everyone mocks me. For when I spoke, I cried out; I shouted, "Violence and plunder!" Because the word of the LORD was made to me a reproach and a derision daily. Then I said, "I will not make mention of Him, nor speak anymore in His name." But His word*

> *was in my heart like a burning fire shut up in my bones; I was weary of holding it back, and I could not.*
> *- Jeremiah 20:7-9*

In the fullness of time - 42 generations from Abraham to David to Jesus - *Jesus* was tagged IT.

> *For unto us a Child is born, unto us a Son is given; and the government will be upon His shoulder. And His name will be called Wonderful, Counselor, Mighty God, Everlasting Father, Prince of Peace. Of the increase of His government and peace there will be no end...*
> *- Isaiah 9:6-7a*

In Biblical days, Jesus walked the earth in a dual role: Son of The LORD and Son of Man. As Son of Man, it provides a glimpse into the fulfillment of A Person's assignment. Tagged IT often throws A Person into a dilemma and he or she must decide to remain stagnant or press toward the mark for the prize of fulfillment.

When the appointed time of preparation came for Jesus to be crucified, He requested that the "cup of suffering" pass from Him.

> *He went a little farther and fell on His face, and prayed, saying, "O My Father, if it is possible, let this cup pass from Me; nevertheless, not as I will, but as You will."   - Matthew 26:39*

If not Him, who? If not then, when? Jesus remembered for that reason was He sent to earth.

> *Again, a second time, He went away and prayed, saying, "O My Father, if this cup cannot pass away from Me unless I drink it, your will be done."*
> *- Matthew 26:42*

> *Therefore, God also has highly exalted Him and given Him the name which is above every name, that at the name of Jesus every knee should bow, of those in heaven, and of those on earth, and of those under the earth, and that every tongue should confess that Jesus Christ is Lord, to the glory of God the Father.*
> *- Philippians 2:9-11*

Take One for the Team

Therefore we also, since we are surrounded by so great a cloud of witnesses, let us lay aside every weight, and the sin which so easily ensnares us, and

let us run with endurance the race that is set before us, looking unto Jesus, the author and finisher of our faith who for the joy that was set before Him endured the cross, despising the shame, and has sat down at the right hand of the throne of God.
- Hebrews 12:1-2

The writer of the Book of Hebrews, the Apostle Paul, admonishes A Person to be aware of his or her surroundings. A specific Person is not the first nor the last to be tagged, IT. There is a large group of believers, heroes and she-roes of the faith, in the virtual stands. They are observing and cheering others on as IT.

Paul was strategic in his writing to new players of the game, "Tag, You're IT." His advice was to look unto Jesus as an example of how to overcome adversity and to stay the course. The goal is to meditate on the person, place or thing that brings joy. *A hater does not have to become a motivator; employ joy.* Supernatural strength will be obtained for comebacks in times of setups and setbacks. A Person must remain persistent even in times of shame, disdain, or pain. It may mean shifting to the sidelines, everybody and everything that attempts to change the rules of the game for their or its comfort. Do not make a permanent decision based on a temporary setback. It will further delay or forfeit a turnaround.

> *For I am already being poured out as a drink offering, and the time of my departure is at hand. I have fought the good fight, I have finished the race, I have kept the faith. Finally, there is laid up for me the crown of righteousness, which the Lord, the righteous Judge, will give to me on that Day, and not to me only, but also to all who have loved His appearing.*
>
> *- 2 Timothy 4:6-8*

> *His lord said to him, "Well done, good and faithful servant; you have been faithful over a few things, I will make you ruler over many things. Enter into the joy of your lord."*
>
> *- Matthew 25:23*

As "A Person," *Spinderella* reminds you that you were born during an era for a specific purpose. Your purpose may not be to build an ark like Noah; become the father of many nations like Abraham; preserve the lives of generations and nations like Joseph; deliver The LORD's chosen people from a taskmaster as Moses did; or be crucified, dead and buried and risen as Jesus was, but your life and assignment matters. You are a small piece in a universal puzzle that The LORD is assembling. Life's challenging experiences may have left you with jagged edges. In the end, you will see that those experiences are what developed and shaped you to fit perfectly into the vacant space in the puzzle.

You can no longer hide in the crowd as a "tag along," nor go along to get along. As The LORD's prophetic mouthpiece, I proclaim to you today, if you did not know it before, you surely do now--- "Tag, You're IT!"

CHAPTER 2

Deal with IT

...A thorn in the flesh was given to me...Concerning this thing I pleaded with the Lord three times that it might depart from me. And He said to me, "My grace is sufficient for you, for My strength is made perfect in weakness." Therefore, most gladly I will rather boast in my infirmities, that the power of Christ may rest upon me.
- 2 Corinthians 12:7-9

Without consent, you were drafted into life's game of "Tag, You're IT." Not only are YOU IT, as you develop and launch into your purpose, you HAVE an IT.

IT is "A Problem" that requires a solution. For some people, little effort is needed to change a vehicle, job, house or spouse. When it comes to certain levels and intensities of an IT, it requires involvement from The Problem Solver to convert a mess into a message and a test into a testimony.

Let's face it. If you do not deal with your IT, IT will deal with you. Collinsdictonary.com states the following about the word, "deal": "When you deal with something or someone that needs attention, you give attention to them, and often solve a problem or make a decision concerning them." It is impossible to deal with something or someone that is not a concern of yours. If you become *uninvolved* with seeking a resolution, your IT will remain *unresolved*.

I will never forget New Year's Day, January 1, 2011. I was reminiscing over a tough, life-changing experience. I heard The LORD say these words to me:

"What you tolerate will continue and will strengthen itself. If you are ready to deal with IT, I AM ready to deal with IT..."

I learned valuable lessons that year and the years that followed while awaiting a turnaround of my IT. Those lessons provided insight into the inner turmoil that *Spinderella* most likely endured during her process to resolve her IT.

My IT was an unmerited demotion. Sometimes, "A Problem" multiplies into additional problems. The demotion included a significant loss of pay.

The process started in March 2007. I received the following prophecy from Archbishop E. Bernard Jordan of New York:

> *Jordan:* Where do you work?
> *Me:* City of Tallahassee.
> *Jordan:* How long have you been there?
> *Me:* 18 years.
> *Jordan:* That season is up. That is

*the end...because there is something
that you are to impart into people.*

Seventeen months later, the prophecy became my reality. I was heartbroken to leave my City work-family after 19 years of employment, but excited about the new door of opportunity. The start date was August 1, 2008. The "eighth" month and the year 2008 represented "new beginnings."

A year later I received a threat of demotion. With my salary of 19 years as a negotiating factor, I accepted the new job for an additional $3,500. The demotion threatened to strip away $15,000 from my annual salary; $1,250 per month! I sought intervention. I felt rejected and forgotten like what was experienced by Joseph in the Book of Genesis (Genesis 40-41:1-44). Often, The LORD, our "Problem Solver," will not allow others to intervene. They may have the power, but not the authority. This is in preparation for when a turnaround occurs, He alone gets the praise.

The demotion and pay cut occurred. This action had become my "IT." In the beginning, IT dealt with me. I could not eat nor sleep. To make matters worse, my son was set to graduate from high school and transition to college-life in another city. Scholarships were minor, and tuition and housing costs were in the major leagues. I was in survival mode and had accumulated a lot of credit card debt to "make ends meet." Due to the drastic pay cut, I did not have a lot of money, but I spent my faith by not withholding an opportunity of higher education for my son to receive a degree in Media Arts and Animation. Thank The LORD, he received his degree and soon, we will see his animations on the big screen and his cartoons, comics and creations worldwide. My strength to press forward came from meditating on the Word of The LORD and building up my prayer life.

> *If you faint in the day of adversity, your strength is small.   - Proverbs 24:10*
>
> *But those who wait on the LORD shall renew their strength; they shall mount up with wings like eagles, they shall run and not be weary, they shall walk and not faint.   - Isaiah 40:31*

I requested prayer from my pastor at that time, Dr. LE Cohen, III. I advised him of the demotion and pay cut and that I would challenge both. At first, I did not want to hear nor receive his response:

"You cannot challenge IT. Let The LORD fight this for you..."

I knew he was a true prophet; therefore, I did not challenge my IT.

Prophetess Francina Norman of Dallas, Texas, prophesied to me in the 1980s. She revealed to me that, "The LORD shows you things before they happen." That is true, and He does so through dreams. Several months after the demotion, I dreamed a flood occurred. It rushed in from ground level to the top floor of an office building. People attempted to escape as they stampeded into the building and ran from the bottom to the top. A few months after the dream of the flood, an unfortunate tragedy occurred. Just like the flood, it created losses from the bottom all the way to the top.

Make God Look Good

A great friend, Prophetess Dr. Delaine Smith, was aware that my soul was troubled about the demotion and pay cut. She ministered to me these words: *"Angie, you got to make God look good!"* I had another dream. It provoked me to guard my heart, character, and The LORD's reputation through my actions and reactions. Throughout the process, The LORD revealed to me that His grace was enough, and His strength was made perfect in my weakness.

> *...A thorn in the flesh was given to me...Concerning this thing I pleaded with the Lord three times that it might depart from me. And He said to me, "My grace is sufficient for you, for My strength is made perfect in weakness." Therefore, most gladly I will rather boast in my infirmities, that the power of Christ may rest upon me.   - 2 Corinthians 12:7-9*

When I was awakened from the dream, I immediately remembered, "*Angie, you got to make God look good!*" The scriptures below came to mind:

> *Be angry, and do not sin: do not let the sun go down on your wrath, nor give place to the devil. - Ephesians 4:26-27*

> *Do not fret because of evildoers, nor be envious of the workers of iniquity. For they shall soon be cut down like the grass, and wither as the green herb. Trust in the LORD, and do good; dwell in the land, and feed on His faithfulness. Delight yourself also in the LORD, and He shall give you the desires of your heart. Commit your way to the LORD, trust also in Him, and He shall bring it to pass. He shall bring forth your righteousness as the light, and your justice as the noonday. Rest in the LORD and wait patiently for Him; do not fret because of him who prospers in his way, because of the man who brings wicked schemes to pass. Cease from anger and forsake wrath; do not fret - it only causes harm.*
>
> *- Psalm 37:1-8*

PIVOTAL MOMENT
We must control our emotions or
our emotions will control us.
- Anonymous

To keep my emotions balanced naturally as well as spiritually, I visited my general practitioner to discuss the demotion and its effects. To be honest, when I thought about the offenses and consequences, I was angry and hurt. As I reflected on my IT, I also felt helpless, but never lost hope that The LORD could not and would not turn IT around. My relationship with Him and His Word strengthened me, again and again, when my soul (mind, will and emotions) was overwhelmed.

> *From the end of the earth I will cry to You, when my heart is overwhelmed; lead me to the rock that is higher than I.*
> *- Psalm 61:2*
>
> *You will keep him in perfect peace, whose mind is stayed on You, because he trusts You. - Isaiah 26:3.*
>
> *We are hard-pressed on every side, yet not crushed; we are perplexed, but not in despair; persecuted, but not forsaken; struck down, but not destroyed." - 2 Corinthians 4:8-9*

> *Looking unto Jesus, the author and finisher of our faith*, who for the joy that was set before Him endured the cross, *despising the shame, and has sat down at the right hand of the throne of God.*
> - Hebrews 12:2

I learned how to forgive and live past the pain. This power came from looking unto Jesus as an example of how to endure hardship and to make it out and on the other side of through. Throughout the years, I have shared the power of Hebrews 12:2 with many people facing A Problem: "Whatever it is that promotes joy, keep that before your eyes." They, too, were strengthened as they meditated on the object that promoted joy instead of focusing on the negativity of their IT.

The Proving Process

I prayed for a turnaround. At times, it appeared that my prayers were not reaching The LORD's throne. The prayer had become a question instead of a request: "Why did this happen to me?" I was puzzled. I am not boasting, but I was (still am) a tither and sower of seeds. Not that I had to, but I reminded The LORD that tithing is not something that I do it is who I am. I am a tither. I also brought to His attention what His Word says about a tither.

> *Bring all the tithes into the storehouse, that there may be food in My house,*

and try Me now in this," says the LORD of hosts, "If I will not open for you the windows of heaven and pour out for you such blessing that there will not be room enough to receive it. And I will rebuke the devourer for your sakes, so that he will not destroy the fruit of your ground...   - Malachi 3:10-11

I shared with Dr. Cohen what I stated to The LORD: "LORD, you have to do something. Not only are my tithes less, but your tithes will be less." Dr. Cohen's response was, "Just because your tithes were cut, does not mean you cut The LORD's tithes. Keep giving the same amount and trust Him." With my faith on trial, I continued giving tithes and offerings as if there had not been an interruption in pay. The process strengthened the sowing of my seeds and faith.

Sow IT and Grow IT or Spend IT and End IT.
- Angie

The LORD downloaded into my spirit, "your salary might be fixed, for now, but your income is not." His scriptures came alive as I also gave alms to those who were less fortunate than me. What a great feeling it was that even though I was in need, to have provided food or an amount as small as $5.00 in the name of Jesus to someone with a greater need, brought peace and joy to my soul. I was already a "cheerful giver," but to give when there is lack is a greater testament of faith and "In God We Trust."

> *He who has pity on the poor lends to the LORD, And He will pay back what he has given.   - Proverbs 19:17*

> *And He looked up and saw the rich putting their gifts into the treasury, and He saw also a certain poor widow putting in two mites. So, He said, "Truly I say to you that this poor widow has put in more than all; for all these out of their abundance have put in offerings for God, but she out of her poverty put in all the livelihood that she had."   - Luke 2:1-4*

A Tight Place

In addition to the demotion, I was advised that I would have to vacate the office that I worked in. The space I was to move into was a thin, cylinder-shaped enclave on the outside of my office.

I had an upcoming preaching service to prepare for. The LORD gave me a message entitled, *"Pressurize Your House."* It was right on time with what had transpired. I was the "house" that needed strengthening with "pressure treated" wood.

I learned that pressure treated wood is used to protect and fortify property from the outside elements. For wood to become "pressurized," it is placed into a tight cylinder and preservatives are squeezed deep into it. I became excited and welcomed the move from the office to the tight place! I said to myself, *"Okay, LORD. I see what you are doing by allowing me to be squeezed into a tight place. It is to infuse a greater intensity of Your anointing not on me but in me."* This infusion would also protect me from the outside elements that tried to infiltrate my heart and soul.

I was transferred and did not have to vacate the office. I was somewhat disappointed because I had prepared mentally to shift into the "tight place." The mental shift was attributed to not just a positive attitude, but a constructive one.

> *"People with a positive attitude hope for the best. People with a constructive attitude make the best of what they've got in order to get closer to where they want to be."* [6]

> *"...So rather than letting those forces control you, realize that you have the*

---

[6] Jakes, T.D. *SOAR*. New York: FaithWords, First Edition: October 2017 (p. 159)

> *power to master your emotions, to step out of suffering and to live the life you want. Because when it comes down to it, we may not be able to control the events that happen in the world, but we do get to decide how we respond to it."*
> — Tony Robbins

Be Not Weary in Well Doing

Changes in leadership led to me being restored to the original position. Restoration of pay was denied. To maintain a constructive attitude throughout the process, I had learned to work as unto The LORD.

> *Work with enthusiasm, as though you were working for the Lord rather than for people.* — Ephesians 6:7

> *And whatsoever you do, do it heartily, as to the Lord and not to men.* — Colossians 3:23

> *"When you step into uncertainty knowing that certainty isn't just a feeling - it's a habit you create - everything shifts. When you have faith and let go of what you can't control and instead put all your focus into what you can make happen, you're on the right path. Whenever you consciously focus on what you have instead of what's*

> *missing, your mind and heart will fill up with gratitude. If you take your focus away from imagined worst-case scenarios and instead focus on serving something or someone you love or something greater than yourself, fear and suffering evaporate. If you truly connect and contribute deeply to something more than just yourself, you will find yourself thriving even in the most turbulent of times."*
> *- Tony Robbins*

I wanted the process to restore my salary to be over quickly. Quickly did not come fast, nor was it in a hurry. It was a five-year ordeal. The LORD placed me on the job, as Archbishop Jordan prophesied, "to impart something into people." I see now that part of the impartation is to share with others that, *"You may not be the cause of A Problem, but it is your responsibility how you respond to IT."*

I received a prophecy from Prophetess Dr. Shaun Carter of Palm Coast, Florida. She was unaware of the demotion and pay cut. She prophesied to congregants. She then turned to me and stated that I would be getting a raise and named the amount. I was shocked! Honestly, it was almost hard to believe, especially knowing the resistance that I encountered. Again, having come through this process, another lesson to impart into others is the following:

Persistence Wears Out Resistance From Man ---
AND THE LORD!
- Angie

The LORD had not provided immediate relief that was tangible. But my persistent faith kept the prophecies coming of what He had in mind for me. If He said it (through His prophetic mouthpiece), I believed that it would come to pass.

> *But he who prophesies speaks edification and exhortation and comfort to men. - 1 Corinthians 14:3*
>
> *God is not a man, that He should lie, nor a son of man, that He should repent. Has He said, and will He not do? Or has He spoken, and will He not make it good? - Numbers 23:19*
>
> *For I know the thoughts that I think toward you, says the LORD, thoughts of peace and not of evil, to give you a future and a hope. - Jeremiah 29:11*

He Turned IT

You have turned for me my mourning into dancing; You have put off my sackcloth and clothed me with gladness, to the end that my glory may sing praise to You and not be silent. O LORD my God, I will give thanks to You forever.   - Psalm 30:11-12

I saw the hand of The LORD at work behind the scenes. When your turn comes up on His appointment calendar, prophets show up to reveal what was concealed. Prophet Daniel Amoateng of London visited our church. He prophesied to me a specific date in September to wear "white." I thought to myself (as the world has groomed us to think), "it is not proper to wear white after Labor Day." However, man's laws do not supersede The LORD's instructions.

A new leader was hired that July. Just as Prophet Amoateng instructed, on the date that he gave me in September, I wore "white white." I looked like a nurse: a white jacket, white dress, and white shoes. A series of events occurred. Afterward, my salary turned, just as Prophetess Carter had prophesied.

When I shifted from my former job to a new one, I was unaware of the twists and turns that awaited my arrival. I share my story to strengthen you who are at the beginning, middle or ending of your IT. The LORD will not allow more to come upon you than you can bear. Do not give up nor out. IT is working together for your good and His glory.

I know that you are praying, "LORD, move on my behalf; turn IT LORD!" The reality is, He may not turn IT, so you will not have to deal with IT. He is always on time, but it appears that He does not show up until you are about to give up or out. The most powerful and unforgettable turn occurs when you are right in the center of IT, with witnesses watching:

> *And these three men, Shadrach, Meshach, and Abed-Nego, fell down bound into the midst of the burning fiery furnace. Then King Nebuchadnezzar was astonished; and he rose in haste and spoke, saying to his counselors, "Did we not cast three men bound into the midst of the fire?" They answered and said to the king, "True, O king." "Look!" he answered, "I see four men loose, walking in the midst of the fire; and they are not hurt, and the form of the fourth is like the Son of God." Then Nebuchadnezzar went near the mouth of the burning fiery furnace and spoke, saying, "Shadrach, Meshach, and Abed-Nego, servants of the Most High God, come out, and come here." Then Shadrach, Meshach, and Abed-Nego came from the midst of the fire. And the satraps, administrators, governors, and the king's counselors*

gathered together, and they saw these men on whose bodies the fire had no power; the hair of their head was not singed nor were their garments affected, and the smell of fire was not on them.

- Daniel 3:23-27

For we have heard how the LORD dried up the water of the Red Sea for you when you came out of Egypt, and what you did to the two kings of the Amorites...And as soon as we heard these things, our hearts melted; neither did there remain any more courage in anyone because of you, for the LORD your God, He is God in heaven above and on earth beneath.

- Joshua 2:10-11

Be encouraged that you have what it takes to see your IT to the end. Deal with IT or IT will deal with you and sabotage your current and future endeavors. Reflect on the words from The LORD that I shared at the beginning of this chapter:

"What you tolerate will continue and will strengthen itself. If you are ready to deal with IT, I AM ready to deal with IT..."

There is great joy, glory, and strength when you deal with your IT.

> *But may the God of all grace, who called us to His eternal glory by Christ Jesus, after you have suffered a while, perfect, establish, strengthen, and settle you.*
> *- 1 Peter 5:10*

> *Beloved, think it not strange concerning the fiery trial which is to try you, as though some strange thing happened unto you: but rejoice, inasmuch as ye are partakers of Christ's sufferings; that, when his glory shall be revealed, ye may be glad also with exceeding joy.*
> *- 1 Peter 4:12-13*

Like *Spinderella* and me, tagged IT at times appear unfair judging by a fiery trial that you did not bring upon yourself. You are the person that The LORD knew could handle and carry out the purpose that you were tagged to fulfill. He is with you every step of the way. When it appears that you can no longer sense Him walking beside you, perhaps He has shifted from beside you to carrying you.

There is preparation before manifestation. Your IT is the very thing that The LORD will use to transition you from where you are to where you are ordained to be and to do.

IT is what IT is, but IT does not have to remain as is. Deal with IT - through prayer and a constructive attitude - or IT will deal with you.

-A Problem-

A situation, person, or thing that needs attention and needs to be dealt with or solved. [7]

It's Infective

To affect by transmission or be communicated to. Used of an idea, emotion, or attitude. [8]

To pass a "dis-ease" to a person.

---

[7] "Definition of 'Problem' - English Dictionary." *Cambridge Dictionary*, dictionary.cambridge.org/us/dictionary/english/problem.

[8] "infect." American Heritage® Dictionary of the English Language, Fifth Edition. 2011. Houghton Mifflin Harcourt Publishing Company 9 Jan. 2019 http://www.thefreedictionary.com/infect

CHAPTER 3

You've Got Me Going in Circles

And the LORD spake unto me, saying, ye have compassed this mountain long enough: turn you northward.   *- Deuteronomy 2:2-3*

What child can resist the sights and sounds of a bright shiny merry-go-round at an amusement park? What parent does not like that it is their child's favorite ride and an opportunity to rest tired feet? Wiktionary defines a merry-go-round as a pleasure ride consisting of a slowly revolving circular platform affixed with various types of seats. It can be a gratifying ride for some, but not all.

In *Spinderella's* case, her adversary was entertained by a metaphoric ride that kept *Spinderella* going in circles. When the ride slowed down for *Spinderella's* exit, more coins were dropped into the token box. The revolving device was constructed to impede her productivity. It had become a major distraction.

The distraction came to prevent her from giving attention to the petition she had before The LORD. Within the word, "distraction," you have 'dis' and 'traction.' Dis means asunder; to divide. Traction is the grip of power felt when the rubber of a vehicle's tire meets the road. When the adversary kept *Spinderella* distracted, her reactions lead to no actions. The commotion caused her not to get a grip on her emotions and her life. The cycle repeated itself year by year at Shiloh.

You are reading this book. For years, you knew something, or someone was agitating or controlling your thoughts, but you could not pinpoint it as a distraction until now. Isn't it time to pull the life support plug from their makeshift merry-go-round connected to the wall of your mind? It existed to impede your productivity. The turn of events that you have been awaiting requires a move of faith. Mike Murdock says, "You cannot conquer what you do not know that you need to confront." Once recognized, identification leads to annihilation. Annihilation becomes elimination.

Spinderella encountered two distracting hindrances while awaiting a turnaround of her IT. They were the spiritual forces of *Resentment and Contentment.* These two spirits manifested in those who resided in the house with her.

Resentment

The late great Nelson Mandela stated that, "No one is born hating another person because of the color of his skin, or his background, or his religion. People must learn to hate, and if they can learn to hate, they can be taught to love, for love comes more naturally to the human heart than its opposite."

Elkanah, chronicled in the Book of 1 Samuel, had two wives. *Spinderella*, whom he celebrated, but she could not have children. And, Peninnah, whom he tolerated, was the other wife. Together, they had a bountiful harvest of children.

> *And when the time was that Elkanah offered, he gave to Peninnah his wife, and to all her sons and her daughters, portions: but unto Hannah he gave a worthy portion; for he loved Hannah: but the LORD had shut up her womb. And her adversary also provoked her sore, for to make her fret, because the LORD had shut up her womb.*
> *- 1 Samuel 1:5-6*

Peninnah's calloused dislike of *Spinderella* had grown into resentment. The hostility was partly due to what Peninnah saw as unfair treatment and disrespect. Their husband's open display of affection towards *Spinderella* was the catalyst. *Spinderella* did not cause Peninnah's alleged injustice of unfair treatment and disrespect. But she was certainly blamed for it due to the appearance that she was highly favored by their husband at Peninnah's expense. The resentment that Peninnah felt for *Spinderella* had not just taken up residence in her heart. It was seen in her actions. Hurt people hurt other people. As a good opponent, Peninnah knew to attack where there was lack. Women in *Spinderella's* era who could not have children were considered a curse. They were treated as such by those who were able to have children. Her provoking pushed *Spinderella* into a forced fast. She sat still and wept, unable to eat while Peninnah probably laughingly said to her, "pass the peas please."

> *And her adversary also provoked her sore, for to make her fret, because the LORD had shut up her womb. And as he did so year by year, when she went up to the house of the LORD, so she provoked her; therefore, she wept, and did not eat.   - 1 Samuel 1:6-7*

Resentment not dealt with can lead to premeditated and attempted murder. This was seen with Joseph (Genesis 37) and his resentful brothers.

> *Now when they saw him afar off, even before he came near them, they conspired against him to kill him. Then they said to one another, "Look, this dreamer is coming! Come therefore, let us now kill him and cast him into some pit; and we shall say, 'Some wild beast has devoured him.' We shall see what will become of his dreams!"*
> *   - Genesis 37:18-20*

Sometimes a person will pick on another because of insecurities in the thing they highlight in another.

Your adversary has great faith about you in the area that you view as a struggle or deficit. It knows that if you ever tapped into the potential within you, you might surpass him or her and he or she would remain in your shadow - a figment of "their" imagination.

People do not want change to come to you for your condition. They see the potential in you that you cannot see in yourself.

Spinderella is a shining beacon of hope, greatness and forgiveness that you can treat others fairly, even if it is not reciprocated. She should have been resentful of Peninnah who had what she desired the most - a male child.

> *"The final proof of greatness lies in being able to endure criticism without resentment."*
> *- Elbert Hubbard*

> *"Forgiveness is the key that unlocks the door of resentment and the handcuffs of hatred. It is a power that breaks the chains of bitterness and the shackles of selfishness."*
> *- Corrie Ten Boom*

Adversary, Necessary but Temporary

To everything there is a season, and a time to every purpose under the heaven.
- Ecclesiastes 3:1

When the devil had ended all the temptation, he departed from him for a season.
- Luke 4:13

The Bible references Peninnah as *Spinderella's* "adversary." Believe it or not, The LORD orders or allows an adversary or adverse situation. Some of you would remain content and not fulfill His will without an adversary stirring you to action. The purpose of your adversary is to provoke you to pay attention to your IT, so you will not quit prior to manifestation.

The Red Sea could not open for the Children of Israel to cross over on dry ground until the Egyptians had come into view to see it. Jesus could not go to the cross and return for His crown until Judas did what he had to do, quickly. Your table will not get prepared before you until it is in the presence of your enemies (Psalm 23).

Like *Spinderella,* your turn was held up all those years until now, the most impactful time. As soon as your adversary has been identified and moved into position, your turn will no longer be delayed nor denied.

Extra! Extra! Read all about it! An adversary is a free advertiser. Their goal is to publicize the area in your life that is viewed as a defect. What they do not realize is IT is what is necessary to perfect you.

> *The LORD will perfect that which concerns me...   - Psalm 138:8*

An adversary arises in your life on purpose and on schedule. Their goal is to kill, steal or destroy you and your reputation. The LORD's plan is that they provoke purpose out of you so that you focus more on His reputation than your own.

Tell your adversary or adverse situation, "You've got me going in circles, but this next go round, my feet will hit the ground running towards my breakthrough not stuck in your ICU. If you do not hurry and do what you purposed in your heart to do against me, I remain delayed in my dilemma. Your provoking is pushing me towards my petition and purpose and further away from the disdain of my pain!"

The good news is, your adversary will expire before your desire does.

Contentment

Then Elkanah her husband said to her, "Hannah, why do you weep? Why do you not eat? And why is your heart grieved? Am I not better to you than ten sons?   - 1 Samuel 1:8

"Congratulations to the proud father of another bouncing boy!" What joy Elkanah had to hear those words again and again. Another son to take with him and his siblings and the men on camping trips. "Time to dust off your pretty in pink clothing. It is another girl!" Who could forget that daddy Elkanah loved his girls? He proudly served as their protector and provider.

That many children were a sign to the people - and *Spinderella* - that Elkanah and his wife, Mother Peninnah, were exceedingly blessed by The LORD.

> *Behold, children are a heritage from the LORD, the fruit of the womb is a reward. Like arrows in the hand of a warrior, so are the children of one's youth. Happy is the man who has his quiver full of them; they shall not be ashamed but shall speak with their enemies in the gate.*
> *- Psalm 127:3-5*

Children are an inheritance, a special possession or portion, given to parents by The LORD. To have one child is to say one is blessed, but a person with a "quiver full of them" is considered greatly blessed. A quiver is a case for holding arrows. Children, represented as "arrows," have the potential to be launched, directed, and instrumental in winning battles if an attack came upon a family.

Children in biblical days were "welfare" and great strength to aging and disabled parents. Boys were regarded highly. They were blessed to carry on the family name from generation to generation. First-born males were chosen as The LORD's.

> *As it is written in the law of The LORD, every male who opens the womb shall be called holy to the Lord.   - Luke 2:23*

This painted a beautiful baby blue canvas for the world to see why Elkanah was completely content. He had his "quiver full of them." It was hard for him to comprehend why *Spinderella* "tripped out" and fretted for not having a child, especially a male child. From his one-sided perspective, he saw himself being better (by what he did) to her than 10 sons.

> *Then Elkanah her husband said to her, "Hannah, why do you weep? Why do you not eat? And why is your heart grieved? Am I not better to you than ten sons?"   - 1 Samuel 1:8*

Spinderella was a wo-man. A woman is created with a womb to give birth. When she did not do what she was designed to do, it created a space within her that could not be filled or satisfied with material possessions. She appreciated her husband's love and gifts. *The gifts pacified her but did not satisfy her need to give birth to his seed.*

> ...*Space, the final frontier. These are the voyages of the starship Enterprise. Its 5-year mission: to explore strange new worlds, to seek out new life and new civilizations,* **to** *boldly go where no man has gone before.* [9]

There is a space inside of a woman that can only be filled and satisfied by a developing embryo.

Was *Spinderella* disappointed with her husband that they could not give birth to a child? I do not believe so. Disappointment comes when an expectation is unfulfilled. He had children with his other wife; therefore, she was aware that he was not the source of her barrenness. I believe Elkanah tried to give *Spinderella* a child. When she did not get pregnant, the impact did not devastate him as it did her. He viewed life through his content lenses. He could physically see his seeds living, moving, and having their little beings. When a person possesses in abundance what another must petition The LORD for, it is hard to comprehend dissatisfaction with lack.

---

[9] "Quotes from 'Star Trek.'" *IMDb*, IMDb.com, www.imdb.com/title/tt0060028/quotes.

A content person is easy to spot. They are predictable and can be counted on to remain normal. They ask the following questions: "Why do you want to go back to school? Why do you need another job? Why do you need to lose more weight? What is wrong with the size that you are now?" It confuses them why you are unhappy with where you are and what you have not accomplished. A content person wants his or her subject of attention to remain consistent. If consistency is misplaced, it frustrates their pattern of control.

Darius Doc D Baker
July 1, 2018
Facebook Post
"Some folks are happy with your stagnation. If you are doing the same things, working the same job, looking the same way, THEY are comfortable. The truth of the matter is that these people sometimes may believe in you more than you believe in yourself! Funny, but it's true and they fear your potential. You must watch folks who give a negative reaction to your positive change. I keep saying, when people say, "You've changed," make sure you know where they are coming from with that. Someone can stop using drugs and their friends (who still use) can say in a negative way," she/he has changed." If you want to see who your true friends are, start doing better for yourself. Some people won't help you because they don't want you to advance more than them! THEY

see your potential, but YOU don't. So, they are your friend if you stay at the same job, drive the same car, stay an employee instead of an employer, live in the same house, remain single all your life, don't do anything to better your appearance, keep the same level of education and so on... As soon as you start trusting God, making positive changes and getting positive results... watch folks carefully 😊: Today I tell you that you've let your "comfort zone" hold you captive for too long and it's time to get all the blessings that God truly has for you. God did not design us to be in the same place year after year. "What got you here, won't get you there" is a quote that I truly believe. You are going to have to change up some things in order to get those greater blessings! You'd already have them if what you've been doing was working. Trust God be confident in yourself and start making positive changes. Say "bye" to stagnation and folks who don't like it, pray for them. Trust me on this, "Know your potential because your enemies do." - Doc D

If *Spinderella* became content as her husband desired, her contentment may have switched to resentment towards him during times of family fellowship and fun.

> *"It isn't what you have or who you are or where you are or what you are doing that makes you happy or unhappy. It is*

what you think about it."
- Dale Carnegie

If you remain steadfast and immovable on the merry-go-round that someone custom ordered for you, you may as well sit back, prop up your feet on the carousel from hell, and quit daydreaming today of a different tomorrow.

The thing that you are pursuing is pursuing you. The accomplishment of your goal requires persistence in times of resistance from those operating in the spirits of resentment and contentment.

"If you want something you have never had,
you must be willing to do something
you have never done."
- Mike Murdock

CHAPTER 4

New Outlook + New Approach = Change

"The awareness of exactly what we are currently doing provides the opportunity for new choices and thus for change."
                                                    - Tony Robbins

Insanity is described as repeating the same thing and expecting a different result. If this description is accurate, *Spinderella's* reactions year by year secured her election as the poster child for insanity.

> *And her adversary also provoked her sore, for to make her fret, because the LORD had shut up her womb. And as he did so year by year, when she went up to the house of the LORD, so she provoked her therefore she wept, and did not eat.   - 1 Samuel 1:6-7*

When a mind lacks clarity and the people in the environment discourages instead of encourages, it leaves no room for new thoughts. New thoughts lead to new behaviors. New behaviors promote new outcomes.

Those who knew and watched *Spinderella* were accustomed to her annual routine: distressed, cried and probably would have died in coming years from not eating. She was a habitual offender. To the eye, it appeared that she sat helplessly at the dinner table and took all that Peninnah dished out of her mouth. Stay tuned.

That year was unlike the rest. What they could not see and hear was the conversation that she had within herself as she "came to herself." This paradigm shift in thinking was an effective tool when the "Prodigal Son's" review of his condition, reconditioned his mind and ultimately his life.

> *But when he had spent all, there arose a severe famine in that land; and he began to be in want. Then he went and joined himself to a citizen of that country, and he sent him into his fields to feed swine. And he would gladly have filled his stomach with the pods that the swine ate, and no one gave him anything.* But when he came to himself, he said, "How many of my father's hired servants have bread enough and to spare, and I perish with hunger? I will arise and go to my father, *and will say to him, Father, I have sinned against heaven, and before you, and I am no longer worthy to be called your son. Make me like one of your hired servants." And he arose and came to his father. But when he was still a great way off, his father saw him, and had compassion, and ran and fell on his neck*

> *and kissed him. And the son said to him, "Father, I have sinned against heaven and in your sight, and am no longer worthy to be called your son." But the father said to his servants, "Bring out the best robe and put it on him; and put a ring on his hand and sandals on his feet. And bring the fatted calf here and kill it and let us eat and be merry; for this my son was dead and is alive again; he was lost and is found." And they began to be merry.*
> *Luke 15:14-24*

A paradigm shift occurs when there is a change in approach. It is an important change that happens when the usual way of thinking about or doing something is replaced by a new and different way. This discovery will bring about a paradigm shift. [10]

She did not, could not eat, but was fed up from repeated cycles in the house of worship. That particular year, she shocked those around her when her new outlook changed her outward approach - she *stood up* for herself!

> *So Hannah **arose** after they had finished eating and drinking in Shiloh.*
> *- 1 Samuel 1:9*

---

[10] Merriam-webster.com.

PIVOTAL MOMENT
If You Can Think Your Way Up,
You Can Think Your Way Out!
- Archbishop E. Bernard Jordan

Hannah first "rose up" in her mind. When the picture in her mind changed, her behavior and reality changed. The new picture she saw helped her to comprehend also that all those years, she had been looking to people to help her who were not equipped to do so. If the LORD "shut up" her womb, He had the power to lose it and let it go to grow fruit after her husband's kind. Please discontinue wasting time and energy talking about your IT to people who are not equipped or empowered to bring change, nor eager for your resolve.

Meditation is your Medication

Sometimes, it is as simple as sitting still and meditating on your IT to promote a favorable change in your direction. Archbishop Jordan states that, "meditation is your medication." With meditation, drugs are not needed nor included. Meditation is a practice where an individual uses a technique, such as focusing their mind on an object, thought or activity, to achieve a mentally clear and emotionally calm state. [11] It is a stress and anxiety reducer and promotes peace and a new perception.

PEACE:
Positively Expect A Calm Ending
Patiently Expect A Calm Ending
- Angie

If you can think your way up, you can think your way out of any situation or condition. *Spinderella* thought her way up and out of the stinking thinking that grounded her for years. Once her mind shifted and no longer drifted, she could not remain stagnant at the table with the spirits of resentment and contentment.

All those years passed, and nothing changed until she changed her perception and approach. She was respectful and waited until the family finished their meals. Afterwards, she rose up. This broke the cycle and destroyed the yokes of her yesterdays. By meditating on a bright future, it released her from a dark past.

---

[11] "Meditation." *Wikipedia*, Wikimedia Foundation, 6 Jan. 2019, en.m.wikipedia.org/wiki/Meditation.

When You Can't Say IT, Pray IT

So, Hannah rose up after they had eaten in Shiloh, and after they had drunk. Now Eli the priest sat upon a seat by a post of the temple of the LORD. And she was in bitterness of soul, and prayed unto the LORD, and wept sore.   - 1 Samuel 1:9-10

Would you take your clothes to a car wash instead of a dry cleaner to be laundered? What about your child to an animal shelter versus a day care center? So, for spiritual guidance, why do you take your personal business to people who do not have a prayer life?

Some things are taught. Others are caught. *Spinderella* caught hold of a revelation. If it was The LORD who shut up her womb, it would be The LORD with the power to open her womb. That year, she did not remain stuck at the table with her husband and her adversary. She took her IT to her LORD in prayer.

> *Casting all your care upon Him, for He cares for you.   - 1 Peter 5:7*

Prayer is communicating with The LORD. There are things that you can say in prayer that are hard to articulate into words.

> *Likewise the Spirit also helps in our weaknesses. For we do not know what we should pray for as we ought, but the Spirit Himself makes intercession for us*

> *with groanings which cannot be uttered.*   *- Romans 8:26*

Earthly License for Heavenly Interference

Not that He needs it, but prayer is us giving The LORD authorization for demonstration into our affairs. The late great Dr. Myles Munroe had this to say about prayer: *It is an "...Earthly license for heavenly interference."* Interference leads to intervention. It is the blocking of an opponent to clear the way for the subject to succeed.

Most of you were told to pray but were not informed what to say. Jesus' Disciples saw and heard Him praying. They did not wait until He asked them if they knew how to pray, they requested of Him to teach them how to pray.

> *Now it came to pass, as He was praying in a certain place, when He ceased, that one of His disciples said to him, "Lord, teach us to pray, as John also taught his disciples."*   *- Luke 11:1*

Prayer is purpose *driven*. It allows access and is our "license" to drive in the spirit realm. A license is a permit from an authority to own or do a thing. The Disciples desired to acquire and to develop skill in praying as John taught his disciples to pray. Evidently, they saw results from a life of prayer. The Master

Instructor, Jesus, took them on a road trip in the realm of the spirit. They remained under his leadership and advanced from a supervised learner's permit; to unsupervised driving; to a standard driver's license; and, excelled to a commercial driver's license (CDL). The CDL equipped them to begin to transport and to train others how to maneuver in the spirit realm.

> *Most assuredly, I say to you, he who believes in Me, the works that I do he will do also; and greater works than these he will do, because I go to My Father.*   *- John 14:12*

She Vowed a Vow

Then she made a vow and said, "O LORD of hosts, if You will indeed look on the affliction of Your maidservant and remember me, and not forget Your maidservant, but will give Your maidservant a male child, then I will give him to the LORD all the days of his life, and no razor shall come upon his head."
- 1 Samuel 1:11

There are trillions of daily prayers that go up to the throne of The LORD. The question is, how many of them get answered?

Praying is essential for strength and growth. Daniel in the Bible prayed three times a day. Jesus prayed consistently and diligently. *Spinderella* was familiar with the power of prayer. The day of her awakening to a new way of seeing and doing things, she added an extra ingredient to her prayer request - she made a vow. It was a sincere oath to The LORD. If He would pay attention to her problem, remembered and granted her petition for a male child, she would give him back and keep him sanctified unto Him.

Many people have made and broken vows as soon as they received their heart's desires. *Spinderella* captured The LORD's attention when she vowed to return to Sender, the male child that she prayed for, year by year. She had tapped into the rhythm of the heartbeat of The LORD. She desired a male child. He had a job opening that had not been posted, yet, for a faithful priest.

In that era, Eli, the priest, was passive in restraining his sons from their transgressions in the House of The LORD. They were tagged It as Eli's successors. Their sins destroyed their destinies and lives. It was the catalyst for the premature death of their father, Eli.

Spinderella's vow was unusual. captured the priest's attention and garnered The LORD's intervention.

PIVOTAL MOMENT
A Sincere Vow will Plow thru Residue and
Usher you into Breakthrough! -Angie

A vow, a special ingredient mixed with prayer, serves as an important nugget for when you seek The LORD for resolution of your IT. You should ask yourself the question, "How can resolution of my IT benefit me and The LORD's Kingdom? I know you are God of the universe, but what are Your needs in the earth?" Teamwork makes the dream work. If you are serious about what you just stated, consider adding *Spinderella's* method to your message. I am aware that it is written in the Word of The LORD:

> *When you make a vow to God, do not delay to pay it... Pay what you have vowed* - Better not to vow than to vow and not pay.   *- Ecclesiastes 5:4-5*

Spinderella's vow was sincere and ushered in a new wave of effective strategic planning. It was a crucial element that provoked a turning point in her much-needed turnaround.

Re-member Me

...O LORD of hosts, if You will indeed look on the affliction of Your maidservant and remember me, and not forget Your maidservant   *- 1 Samuel 1:11*

To remember someone or something is deeper than simply an awareness of them or it. *Spinderella* requested of The LORD to "remember me." From her spectrum of being, not only did she feel abandoned, but dis-membered and in need of her members put back together again.

Life happens. At times, it can leave you feeling torn in pieces and scattered abroad like a puzzle game. If it was a puzzle that she felt her life resembled, she had come to the right person - Our Problem Solver - for re-assembly.

Experienced puzzle players start by putting the ends together to build the framework. Wisdom has taught them that the middle part takes more work and time before a completed picture comes into view. The LORD was the Executive Producer behind the scene directing cast members and scripts written to make *Spinderella's* ends come together at the right time and place. He was also working on her upcoming season finale designed as an in-filler and thriller!

He Looked Beyond My Faults

Kindergarteners through 12th graders are the most likely to experience name-calling or fault-finding. It is largely due to imperfections galore during developmental years.

In the Bible, it was people with "faults" that the LORD appear to have "tagged" for impactful life lessons. Moses had a speech impediment, but his voice was used to deliver the children of Israel from Egypt (Exodus 9). A certain woman hemorrhaged for 12 years, but was used to show the people the power of great faith when she touched Jesus and was instantly healed (Luke 8:43-48). Jonathan's son, Mephibosheth, was dropped as a baby, lamed, but was used to reveal the power of covenant (2 Samuel 9:9-17).

The priest Eli would not judge his sons, but he had the audacity to publicly criticize *Spinderella*. He found fault with her for a crime she had not committed. If any fault was to be found, it was in The LORD who had shut up her womb. The "fault" provoked her adversary to harass her. And, now, the harassment escalated to embarrassment administered at the hands of The LORD's priest.

If you surf the Internet, you may have come across Internet sensations wherein victims of prolonged school bullying snapped back, unexpectedly. Many can be viewed punched or pushed as they attempted to walk away from unwarranted confrontations. Bullies who enjoyed the attention of crowds of people, did not forfeit opportunities to make themselves appear invincible.

In opening scenes from live streams, to tormentors of mental or physical abuse, their targets appeared timid and defenseless. When scripts were flipped as you continued watching, bystanders AND BULLIES were seen shocked! Victims responded with blows and acts of bravery at their breaking points. Their reactions stemmed from built-up energy and emotional trauma from weeks, months, and sometimes years of torment. Some torment, attributed to "fault-finding," caused victims to experience an "underground" eruption. *This type of eruption is best described as an "earthquake."*

> An earthquake occurs when energy is suddenly released in the earth's lithosphere: the surface of the earth shakes because of this energy. When this energy is released, it creates seismic waves. Earthquakes can occur *anywhere* within the Earth's crust, but most commonly occur along active plate boundaries. Earthquakes that occur intraplate (within plates) are *usually caused by the reactivation of very old fault systems.*[12]

Fault systems, friction, and a sudden burst of energy traveling through the "earth's" crust are contributors also to a human's earth (body) quake. You can see a similar development building up deep within *Spinderella's core*. Year by year, she was harassed by her adversary, Peninnah. She wept and could not eat.

After she thought her way up and out of a reoccurring cycle, she was next seen in the temple

---

[12] https://socratic.org/questions/what-is-an-earthquake

where she prayed. Even though she moved away from the spot and the people that provoked the same emotional triggers, yearly, her IT remained unresolved. There was still commotion in her emotions and it caused her earth to "quake."

Can you imagine internal grief so intense that words cannot be uttered from the lips of a grieving heart? Unlike some victims of bullying who had taken matters into their own hands, *Spinderella* did not fight back with words nor fists. She took her grief to The LORD in prayer.

> *And she was in bitterness of soul, and prayed to the LORD, and wept in anguish. Now Hannah spoke in her heart; only her lips moved, but her voice was not heard. Therefore, Eli thought she was drunk. So Eli said to her, "How long will you be drunk? Put your wine away from you!" But Hannah answered and said, "No, my lord, I am a woman of a sorrowful spirit. I have drunk neither wine nor intoxicating drink but have poured out my soul before the LORD. Do not consider your maidservant a wicked woman, for out of the abundance of my complaint and grief I have spoken until now."*
> *- 1 Samuel 1:10, 13-16*

While you are going through a "breaking process," the people you thought would understand you will be the ones looking at you from afar. They will not recognize the signs of your distress but will misjudge and mislabel it as "drunkenness or madness."

The LORD allows "natural disasters" to displace, unearth, breakup stuff in us that cannot go with us into our next dimension of being. The commotion is an indication that our miracle is in motion!

> *But may the God of all grace, who called us to His eternal glory by Christ Jesus, after you have suffered a while, perfect, establish, strengthen, and settle you.*
> *- 1 Peter 5:10*

There is a dimension of prayer that you can get to that gets God's attention and yields positive results. It is called, "effective, fervent prayer."

> *Confess your trespasses to one another, and pray for one another, that you may be healed. The effective, fervent prayer of a righteous man avails much.*
> *- James 5:16*

If you are ready for your IT to change, the time has come to change the way you see and respond to IT.

Just when you thought
there was no hope...

-The Problem Solver-

A person who finds solutions to difficult or complex issues.[13]

The Effect

A change which is a result or consequence of an action or other cause.[14]

---

[13] "Problem-Solver | Definition of Problem-Solver in English by Oxford Dictionaries." *Oxford Dictionaries | English*, Oxford Dictionaries, en.oxforddictionaries.com/definition/problem-solver.

[14] "Effect | Definition of Effect in English by Oxford Dictionaries." *Oxford Dictionaries | English*, Oxford Dictionaries, en.oxforddictionaries.com/definition/effect.

He Turned IT | Angie L. Keaton Wiggins

CHAPTER 5

Power of Agreement

Again, I say to you that if two of you agree on earth concerning anything that they ask, it will be done for them by My Father in heaven.   - Matthew 18:19

There is the opportunity to accomplish much when people come into harmony for a common goal. Even if the motive is wrong, the unity makes the objective achievable. Genesis 11 is an example of a people coming together to build a city and tower. The LORD took note that nothing could stop them. If they could think it, they would achieve it. He did not have a problem with them building the city nor tower. He stopped their work because of their reason for building - to make a name for themselves.

> *Now the whole earth had one language and one speech. And they said, "Come, let us build ourselves a city, and a tower whose top is in the heavens; let us make a name for ourselves, lest we be scattered abroad over the face of the whole earth." But the LORD came down to see the city and the tower which the sons of men had built. And the LORD said, "Indeed the people are one and they all have one language, and this is*

> what they begin to do; now nothing that they propose to do will be withheld from them. Come, let Us go down and there confuse their language, that they may not understand one another's speech." So, the LORD scattered them abroad from there over the face of all the earth, and they ceased building the city. - Genesis 11:1, 4-8

If working together worked for those with a wrong motive, certainly it will work for those with a right motive.

Spinderella was unaware that she had been watched by the Priest, Eli. He assumed that she was drunk because she prayed inwardly - her lips moved - but her voice was not heard.

> And she was in bitterness of soul, and prayed unto the LORD, and wept in anguish. Now Hannah spoke in her heart; only her lips moved, but her voice was not heard. Therefore, Eli thought she was drunk. So, Eli said to her, "How long will you be drunk? Put your wine away from you!" But Hannah answered and said, "No, my lord, I am a woman of sorrowful spirit: I have drunk neither wine nor intoxicating drink but have

> *poured out my soul before the LORD.*
> *- 1 Samuel 1:10, 13-16*

In Biblical times, a function of a priest was to act as mediator between The LORD and man. If there was a misunderstanding between *Spinderella* and the priest, nothing would be accomplished. As soon as they cleared up the misunderstanding, the priest came into agreement with her petition. *The power of agreement created harmony and produced a positive effect. It is a good thing to maintain harmonious relationships. You never know who has access to The LORD's ear and can put in a good word on your behalf!*

> *Then Eli answered and said, "Go in peace, and the God of Israel grant your petition which you have asked of Him."*
> *- 1 Samuel 1:17*

One word from The LORD - through the Priest Eli - turned *Spinderella's* frown upside down into a smile.

> *And she said, "Let your maidservant find favor in your sight." So, the woman went her way and ate, and her face was no longer sad.*
> *- 1 Samuel 1:18*

Don't Stop Until IT DROP

"Persistence wears out resistance." - Anonymous

This year, if you are determined to bring resolve to your IT, no opposition, battle, challenge, or adversary can prevent achievement. IT may be delayed, but not denied.

Sometimes, a delay and disappointment occur when you expect resolution from a person, place, or thing that does not have the power to promote change. It could be the right person to assist you, but in the wrong attitude, he or she dismisses you. This scenario occurred in the Bible when a widow went to a judge seeking mercy to help with her IT.

The judge repeatedly denied her plea. The widow troubled his spirit with the same petition when she appeared before him repeatedly. His refusal, facial nor harsh verbal expressions removed her from his presence. The judge talked himself into giving her what she requested. If he did not, she would not be disappearing from the court room no time soon.

> *Then He spoke a parable to them, that men always ought to pray and not lose heart, saying: "There was in a certain city a judge who did not fear God nor regard man. Now there was a widow in that city; and she came to him, saying, 'Get justice for me from my adversary.' And he would not for a while; but afterward he said within himself,*

'Though I do not fear God nor regard man, yet because this widow troubles me I will avenge her, lest by her continual coming she weary me.' Then the Lord said, 'Hear what the unjust judge said. And shall God not avenge His own elect who cry out day and night to Him, though He bears long with them?' - Luke 18:1-7

Many years came and left, but *Spinderella* held fast to her petition. She did so in spite of the resistance from her adversary, her husband, and her LORD.

Until IT DROP

And let us not grow weary while doing good, for in due season we shall reap if we do not lose heart.
- *Galatians 6:9*

Until the time that his word came to pass, the word of the Lord tested him.
- *Psalm 105:19*

Most times, there is a testing before blessing. Tests are administered to assess skills and eligibility. The Prophet Elisha referenced in 2 Kings 2:2 was tested. Would he leave his mentor and forfeit the transference of his mantle? Jesus was tested in the wilderness. Would He give in to Satan's temptations and forfeit His seat on the right hand of the throne of

God and the honor of a name that is above every name?

What did Joseph experience until the dream of his brothers bowing down to him, "DROPPED?" He was thrown in a pit and prison, but kept working as unto The LORD, kept the faith that he would not be confined always, and maintained his integrity and relationship with The LORD. What did *Spinderella* do until her IT "DROPPED?" She continued showing up to the worship service and family meals, even though she was barren and bawling from the attacks of her adversary.

Like Elisha, Joseph, Jesus and *Spinderella*, what do you do until your IT turns? You keep showing up, keep the faith, keep persevering, and keep praying and believing. One day, the Problem Solver will "DROP" in unexpectedly with your "Desire Reaped Over Prayer."

Until then, waiting is not The LORD rejecting you, but allowing patience to have its perfect work in you.

> *But let patience have its perfect work, that you may be perfect and complete, lacking nothing.   - James 1:4*
>
> *I would have lost heart, unless I had believed that I would see the goodness of the LORD in the land of the living. Wait on the LORD; be of good courage,*

and He shall strengthen your heart; wait, I say, on the LORD!
- Psalm 27:13-14

*"It's not where you start,
It's where you end up."
- Anonymous*

CHAPTER 6

He Turned IT

Then they rose early in the morning and worshipped before the LORD, and returned and came to their house at Ramah: and Elkanah knew Hannah his wife; and the LORD remembered her.
- 1 Samuel 1:19

Home is where the heart is. It should be the place where you feel love from all who dwell within its borders.

We witnessed in chapters past, how *Spinderella* and her petition for a male child were belittled in Shiloh. The resentment and contentment from her adversary and spouse did not begin in Shiloh. It started at home then spread abroad.

There is a change in the atmosphere. *Spinderella* looked the same on the outside, but a wonderful change had occurred on the inside. The trip from Shiloh to home was uneventful. The womb of *Spinderella's* mind had been miraculously excavated and cultivated. And, now, she was "open" to receive her husband's seed into fertile ground.

They returned home to Ramah as they had done many years prior. Ramah signifies a height or a high place.[15] All this time, *Spinderella* had been residing in a "high place," but existing as if she was anchored to a bottomless pit. Dr. YaQuanda McCall of Tallahassee, FL, states to callers on her daily 5AM Prayer Calls, "no more low life living!" *Spinderella* and family returned to the high place. This was a prophetic move for her. She had to continue to cultivate the ground of her mind with elevated thoughts of new endeavors on the horizon. She had to guard her heart and mind for when the low life living of the past hauntingly tried to invade her new found thought life.

When you receive a Word of prophesy, you must safeguard it from the environment that you return to. You must cultivate an environment conducive for its matriculation from potential to reality.

In the natural things may look the same, but your outlook changes the landscape of what is seen. There shall be a performance and you are the leading lady or man. It is showtime. Are you ready to go higher than you have been before?

As *Spinderella* requested from The LORD, He "remembered her!"

---

[15] https://wol.jw.org/en/wol/d/r1/lp-e/1200003630. Insight on the Scriptures, Volume 2 p. 731

Asked of God; Heard by God

So it came to pass in the process of time that Hannah conceived and bore a son, and called his name Samuel, saying, "Because I have asked for him from the LORD."   - 1 Samuel 1:20

If you grew up in the 70s and 80s, you probably heard it stated that, "You are not to question God or ask Him for anything." That statement came from a place of religion which was more prevalent back then than a relationship with Him. James 4:2 declares, "...you do not have because you do not ask." The LORD desires that we make our petitions known unto Him.

> *Be anxious for nothing, but in everything by prayer and supplication, with thanksgiving, let your requests be made known to God, and the peace of God, which surpasses all understanding, will guard your hearts and minds through Christ Jesus.*
>
> *- Philippians 4:6-9*

Spinderella was specific and got just what she requested. "a male child." Now, the evidence of her faith was staring her doubters in the face. She named him "Samuel." It means, "asked of God." She requested, and The LORD manifested. She came to the end of her faith, and restoration of her soul.

> *Receiving the end of your faith - the salvation of your souls. - 1 Peter 1:9*

Have you received your IT, since you made your request known? Samuel represents the faith-filled prayers of *Spinderella* who doubted not in her heart. You, too, can come to the end of your faith when the evidence of what you are believing for shows up.

> *For this child I prayed; and the LORD hath given me my petition which I asked of him. - 1 Samuel 1:27*

Shut Up & Open Up

Talk no more so very proudly; let not arrogance come from your mouth, for the LORD is the God of knowledge; and by Him actions are weighed. The bows of the mighty men are broken, and those who stumbled are girded with strength. Those who were full have hired themselves out for bread, and the hungry have ceased to hunger. Even the barren has born seven, and she who has many children has become feeble. - 1 Samuel 2:3-5

If you have spent significant time watching movies, you probably will agree with this summation: At the beginning of a movie, you find yourself shedding tears and talking back to the screen due to the mistreatment or misfortune of the protagonist. But, before the credits scroll across the screen at the end of the movie, you have dried those tears and leaped for joy that the good character may have lost a few battles, but did not lose the war.

> *And let us not grow weary while doing good, for in due season we shall reap if we do not lose heart.*
> *- Galatians 6:9*

The scriptures never recorded that *Spinderella* exchanged hurtful words with Peninnah when she was harassed by her for not having children. It was The LORD who shut up *Spinderella's* womb and it was The LORD who intervened on her behalf.

> *Repay no one evil for evil. Have regard for good things in the sight of all men. If it is possible, as much as depends on you, live peaceably with all men. Beloved, do not avenge yourselves, but rather give place to wrath; for it is written, "Vengeance is Mine, I will repay," says the Lord.*
> *- Romans 12:17-19*

Peninnah's <u>mouth was open</u>, provoking Spinderella, who's <u>womb was closed</u> and unable to bear children. When it was all said and done, there was a swift shift! The LORD <u>shut up</u> Peninnah's mouth and <u>opened up</u> Spinderella's womb! Not only did Peninnah's mouth get shut, her womb did too. She was unable to have more children.

PIVOTAL MOMENT
The LORD SHUT UP Peninnah's Mouth
and OPENED UP *Spinderella's* Womb!
- Angie

Spinderella made good on her vow to give her child back to The LORD. She knew her limitations and put the seed of her priestly/prophetic son back into The LORD's rich soil for the Priest Eli to nurture him for ministry.

The LORD visited her, again, and gave her additional children. Why? Because she made good on the "loan" that she promised she would give to Him. It yielded a high percentage compounded interest rate on her investment!

> *And Eli would bless Elkanah and his wife, and say, "The LORD give you descendants from this woman for the loan that was given to the LORD." Then they would go to their own home. And the LORD visited Hannah, so that she conceived and bore three sons and two daughters. Meanwhile the child Samuel grew before the LORD.*
> *- 1 Samuel 2:20-21*

Like *Spinderella* and me, we were trusted with trouble. She was barren and sought The LORD to be able to deliver. I shared in Chapter 2 how my finances were drastically impacted, and I sought Him for deliverance. When both of our lives were constantly *revolving* in circles and never evolving forward, our common denominator was our persistent faith and confidence in The LORD's providence. We encountered a few twists and setbacks along the way. *Spinderella* and I did not know how nor when, but we knew, The LORD would turn IT around for our good.

> *And we know that all things work together for good to them that love God, to them who are the called according to his purpose.*
> *- Romans 8:28*

It is my prayer that *Spinderella's* and my testimonies, and the testimonials in Chapter 8, promotes your turn of events and provokes you into a greater relationship with The LORD. A relationship that would shift you from simply hearing about Him as God the creator to knowing Him as LORD of your life.

> *I had heard of you by the hearing of the ear, but now my eye sees you.*
> *- Job 42:5 ESV*

Somewhere between the preface and back cover, may your strength and faith be renewed to pursue your turnaround from The LORD. It is your time and your turn - "Tag, You're It!"

All things are possible - if you believe.

Let us Pray:

Our Father in heaven, hallowed be Your name. We thank You for who You are and for what You mean to us. In the name of Jesus, we are grateful for the opportunity to "Come boldly to the throne of grace, that we may obtain mercy and find grace to help in time of need." Thank You in advance for hearing and answering our prayers as they align with Your Holy Word. We declare the decree that testimonies shall come forth from married couples who have been steadfast and unmovable in their quest and request for the birthing of a child. May the life and legacy of Spinderella and the spouses in this book be a source of inspiration and strength to married couples as they wait on You to turn IT around for them. Let this be the year they cheer for answered prayer.

We thank You for healthy pregnancies and babies, and the restoration of marriages, homes and ministries.

We beseech You on behalf of those whose "IT" is a request for healing - mentally, physically, spiritually, financially, and the effects felt in families, ministries, work and marketplaces. We know that Jesus was, "wounded for our transgressions, bruised for our iniquities, the chastisement for our peace was upon Him, and by His stripes we are healed." Therefore, we receive it. We give you praise, honor, and glory.

In the matchless and powerful name of Jesus. Amen.

For with God nothing will be impossible
-Luke 1:37

CHAPTER 7

Spinderella's Prayer of Thanksgiving
(1 Samuel 2:1-10)

And Hannah prayed and said:

My heart rejoices in the LORD; my horn is exalted in the LORD. I smile at my enemies, because I rejoice in Your salvation.

No one is holy like the LORD, for there is none besides You, nor is there any rock like our God.

Talk no more so very proudly; let no arrogance come from your mouth, for the LORD is the God of knowledge; and by Him actions are weighed. The bows of the mighty men are broken, and those who stumbled are girded with strength.

Those who were full have hired themselves out for bread, and the hungry have ceased to hunger. Even the barren has borne seven, and she who has many children has become feeble.

The LORD kills and makes alive; He brings down to the grave and brings up.

The LORD makes poor and makes rich; He brings low and lifts.

He raises the poor from the dust and lifts the beggar from the ash heap, to set them among princes and make them inherit the throne of glory. For the pillars of the earth are the LORD's, and He has set the world upon them.

He will guard the feet of His saints, but the wicked shall be silent in darkness.

For by strength no man shall prevail. The adversaries of the LORD shall be broken in pieces; from heaven He will thunder against them. The LORD will judge the ends of the earth. He will give strength to His King and exalt the horn of His anointed.

No Test - No Testimony!

Therefore, I say to you, whatever things you ask when you pray, believe that you receive them, and you will have them.

- Mark 11:24

CHAPTER 8

Testimonials

There will be Glory...After This

My husband, Eric, and I had been married for two years when we decided to start a family. As you can imagine, we were very excited. It took us almost a year, but we were so overjoyed when we discovered we were pregnant. We were so happy. We shared the news with family members that our family was expanding! But, little did we know that a dark cloud was looming over our elated and elevated cloud nine. Two weeks after my pregnancy was confirmed, my knees buckled underneath me. I felt sharp, stabbing abdominal pains. My worst fears were confirmed when I visited my OB/GYN. We had miscarried.

How could God allow me, His devoted and faithful servant who "did things the right way," to go through something so devastating, so embarrassing, and so cruel? I could not understand it. What possible lesson could God want me to learn from this situation? Because of course, He does want me to learn from this, right? I was in such a state of utter confusion and hurt. I cried out to God for Him to help me heal from this brokenness.

I do not have all the answers of why we as God's children go through certain situations and circumstances. But I do know that our God who promises is faithful!

> *Let us hold fast the confession of our hope without wavering, for He who promised is faithful.* - Hebrews 10:23

God is the Master Architect. He builds, places and/or allows certain trials, tribulations, hurts and disappointments in our lives to mold us into His workmanship that He can get the glory out of. Today, I am a witness that He who promises---IS FAITHFUL!

Scared. Shocked. Confused. Ignorant. Angry. These and other less than positive feelings describe just how Eric and I felt in June 2013 when our sons, Jeremiah Christopher *"Champ"* and Joshua Alexander were born. However, I don't think any words can adequately describe that initial moment when your life drastically changes forever.

SCARED: On the morning of June 25, 2013, approximately 8 a.m., a nurse came into my hospital room to perform my standard ultra-sound to check the heart rate of my twin boys. They were known as Baby A and Baby B. Five minutes after the ultra sound, I noticed that the nurse had a strange expression on her face. She then stated to my husband and I that we would be meeting our little boys sooner than we thought. In no time, at 36½ weeks, I was being prepped for what would later be identified to us as a dramatic C-section. Eric and I said a quick prayer, then called and texted our family that our big day had arrived!

SHOCKED: A swarm of nurses, doctors and specialists filled the operating room. They began working on Jeremiah and Joshua. Unknown to us, Baby B now known as Joshua, had passed away in my womb. Baby A, Jeremiah, was born not breathing. Initially, I was not worried. I felt that whatever was going on, God's got it. Eric and I knew that regardless of the "weapon" that had formed we would prosper and prevail.

> *No weapon formed against you shall prosper...This is the heritage of the servants of the LORD, and their righteousness is from Me, says the LORD.   - Isaiah 54:17*

Because after all, these were God's babies and He would not allow anything to happen to them. When the enemy came in like a flood, I knew that God would lift a standard against him (ref. Isaiah 59:19).

CONFUSED & IGNORANT: Eric and I did not know what was happening to our baby boy. It was discovered that Jeremiah had hypoxic-ischemic encephalopathy (HIE) due to possible trauma in the womb. We were informed that he may have encountered additional complications. Within 45 minutes of delivering my precious twin boys, my husband and I were signing papers to transport our now only son to UF Health Shand's Hospital in Gainesville, FL (2½ hours away). He was transferred there to receive the new hypothermia "cooling" treatment. I did not fully understand what this procedure was...and frankly, I did not care! All I was concerned about was getting my son the best medical treatment for him to receive a fighting chance at life.

ANGRY: So, while I was in Tallahassee, FL, recovering from my C-section and making burial preparations for our stillborn son, Joshua, Jeremiah was miles away from me. He was sedated and undergoing numerous tests and evaluations. I was literally numb. I asked God several times "Why? Why God? Why did this happen to Eric and I? We were pure with each other, and we do not drink or smoke. We both committed our lives to You at an early age and this is how we are rewarded? WHY GOD?" I had so many questions in my mind, but there was a still small voice that whispered back to me that, "God would get the glory out of this." Instantly, my spirit was calmed, and I felt peace.

It was then that I realized that my strategy for getting through this trial was to pray, war in the spirit with His Word and keep the joy of the Lord in my heart. We nervously and desperately stayed by the phone in my room to receive updated reports and pictures of Jeremiah from my aunt and Eric's Mom and Dad. We did not know from call to call what the news would be. Over the course in the NICU III, where the more severe cases are located, Jeremiah had multiple seizures, a blood transfusion, stopped breathing and other complications such as microcephaly.

My twin sister transported my breast milk from Tallahassee to Gainesville to make sure Champ was getting the nutrients he needed to grow stronger. A week later, Eric and I arrived at the hospital. We knew this was not a time to get in our emotions and feel sorry for Jeremiah nor ourselves. We knew that no matter how tragic our experience had been, this was an opportunity for God to show Himself strong!

We walked into the NICU III and began praying not just for Jeremiah, for every baby in there. We spoke to the atmosphere and commanded healing and rebuked death. We prayed for the doctors and nurses. God was working because the day after we arrived, Jeremiah was relocated to the NICU I. The less severe unit. Slowly, we noticed that other babies that were in NICU III were also being transferred to NICU I. Where it was believed that Jeremiah might spend a month or two in the hospital, our Champ was in there for only about 2½ weeks! Our God is a healer!

Today, Jeremiah is an active three-year-old who is reaching and, in some cases, exceeding his developmental milestones. He is not on any medication and God has healed him from microcephaly. To see him running around or trying to help Mommy cook, you would not know he had such a traumatic start. He is truly our miracle baby. So, what do you do when you are faced with a trial or situation that knocks you off your feet and you feel that you cannot go on? You stand still and know that He is God and speak life to your situation. Because, there will be glory...after this!

Amazed by His Grace,
--Shawnda--

Eric, LaShawnda & Jeremiah Swanigan
Photo courtesy of LaShawnda

Birthing Prophecy

I remember it as if it were yesterday, June 2000. I was 29 years old sitting in a cold examination room waiting for the fertility specialist to return. This Caucasian very heavyset man walks in the room, breathing hard and wreaking of cigarette smoke says, "Alicia, it appears that you have premature ovarian failure." With a look of utter confusion on my face, I asked nervously, "What does that mean?" Looking over his glasses he said sternly, yet very matter of fact, "it means that you won't be able to have children. Your body has gone into early menopause, and your ovaries look like that of an 85-year-old woman." I was stunned, numb, shocked, hurt, and in total disbelief. I felt as if he had just told me I only had 30 days to live; it felt like a death sentence. He further stated: "We will call you once we have the results of your hormone levels, but I'm certain that your FSH (follicle stimulating hormone) will come back high, which will confirm your POF (premature ovarian failure)."

Honestly, I don't even remember leaving the doctor's office. That day, bitterness consumed me. I was mad at God. Why would He allow this to happen to me? I'm a good person; I was the most respectful child my mother had; and, I had a giving heart. What did I do that was so bad that I deserved this death sentence? That's what it felt like to me! All I have ever wanted in my life was to have children. But I remembered something that my mother told me at the tender age of seven years old. She looked at me, and she said: "Lisa, you're not going to start having children until what most people consider past your childbearing years." Now I'm seven years old, and I didn't understand what she meant by that and why she was saying that to me. My mother has always told me that I was a very special child. Through all the heartache, hurt, pain, emptiness of my reality of not being able ever to have children, that prophetic word my mother gave me at seven years old never left me! That word would always come back to my remembrance.

After marrying my current husband in 2004, the desire to have a child never went away. It intensified and so did my bitterness. I would use materialistic possessions and alcohol to try to fill my void. There were not enough name brand handbags, shoes, clothes or fancy cars that could fill this void, this emptiness, this pain I carried around and tried to camouflage. I felt defective, and less than a woman. I felt like damaged goods! My faith was on empty! The bitterness caused me to become lethal. I needed to change my life because I was headed down the road to destruction. I hit rock bottom hard!

I begin to go to church, which I was no stranger to me being a PK (preachers' kid). But I was still empty! The desire to have a child would never go away. I can remember asking God, "God why don't you just take this desire away from me?" He never did. I understand now that when God places a desire in your heart, He puts it there because He wants you to go through your process to pursue the promise to manifestation.

February 2018, my husband and I decided to pursue seeing another fertility specialist after being encouraged and supported by our Pastors, Dr. Nicky & Carlos Collins. It was a long and hard process for us. IVF (In Vitro Fertilization) is not for the faint-hearted. God reminded me during this long and sometimes lonely process that had I known that I would have to go through then what He was preparing me to go through now, I would not have been able to handle my "IT"! I remember riding down the road in March 2018, I cried out to The LORD, and I said: "God, I want to be pregnant by Christmas!" There was something that took place in the realm of the spirit that day! My cry activated my faith like never before! The more I wanted to give up the more God reminded me of His promise through that prophetic word my mother spoke over me at seven years old.

On September 27, 2018, my husband and I conceived with our first round of IVF treatment. I'm currently four months pregnant, and we are expecting a beautiful baby in June of 2019! Forty years later, God kept His promise given to a seven-year-old little girl through a prophetic word from her mother.

I'm birthing prophecy! Never give up on the promises of God, no matter how long it takes. Trust that He will do just what He said and His timing will be perfect.

- Lisa Ward

Photo Courtesy of Prophetess Lisa Ward

Prayer Changes IT

I give honor to God and to his beautiful servant, Prophetess Angie Wiggins, for allowing me to share my testimony. It is my prayer that it will encourage others who are going through or have gone through the same trial of barrenness as Hannah (a.k.a. *Spinderella*).

I had two children out of wedlock. My 1995 baby, 23-year-old navy corpsman, Tiarik. And, my now 15-year-old high school daughter, Chelsy.

Fast-forward to 2011. I was 33 years old. I desired to have another child. My former pastor, Dr. LE Cohen, III, prophesied to me that, "God is going to clean out your immune system and prepare your body for a baby." I was so excited because God heard my silent prayers. I was not on birth control; therefore, I thought I would be able to conceive. Not so. Five years had gone by.

I was planning and preparing for my wedding that occurred on December 3, 2016. Full of stress and excitement I conceived, unknowingly. You see, while planning for my big day, I conceived my third pregnancy - out of wedlock, again. I became pregnant in November of 2016. I did not become aware of the pregnancy until mid-December.

January 1, 2017, I went on my honeymoon to the Bahamas. My husband and I were happily married...and pregnant. I will never forget the date of January 7, 2017. It was a cold and freezing day. I was taking a shower at a hotel in Gainesville, FL. I was preparing to walk down the aisle as a bridesmaid in my friend's wedding. I miscarried! My heart miscarried also. I lost all hope and questioned God so many times. I called my mother to share the sad news with her. She responded, "baby I did not want to tell you, but I dreamed you miscarried. It was a little girl. As I held the fetus in the palm of my hands, I stated to you, 'I could put it back together again.'" I inquired of her why she did not share the dream with me earlier. She advised, "Baby I did not want to ruin your happiness." My mom also thought that if she rebuked the dream it would never manifest.

A year after my miscarriage, I dropped to my knees at the side of my bed and gave a heartfelt prayer to God.

> *...The effective, fervent prayer of a righteous man avails much."*
> *- James 5:16*

I said, "Lord I am married now, and I still desire a baby. Lord, You honor marriage, family and unity. You gave your man of God, Dr. Cohen, a word that I would have a baby. Father God, you gave your daughter, Prophetess Soyini Cherry Webbe, a dream that I had delivered a baby. Father God in the name of Jesus, please honor your word Amen and Amen."

On September 7, 2018, I took a pregnancy test and God had honored His word. He implanted His promise into my womb. I am now almost four months pregnant. No complications!

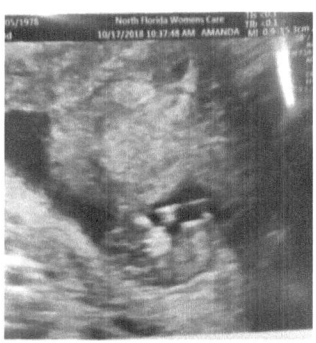

My husband, Shon, and I went to our first O/B appointment. What a blessing it was to watch our baby move and kick. The heartbeat was very strong. I cried tears of joy.

God's timing is not our timing. Catch this, I miscarried January 7, 2017, and I found out that I was pregnant September 7, 2018. Seven is the number of *"completion* and *it is finished.*" We look forward to a healthy pregnancy and birth. We give God praise that He kept His word and He turned our "IT" around for our good.

> *God is not a man, that He should lie, nor a son of man, that He should repent. Has He said, and will He not do? Or has He spoken, and will He not make it good?* - Numbers 23:19

Shon and Chanel Wiley White & Family
Photos courtesy of Chanel Wiley White

If The LORD Said IT You Can Count On IT

But he who prophesies speaks edification and exhortation and comfort to men.
- 1 Corinthians 14:3

I preached several years ago at a church in my hometown. While preaching, I received a prophetic utterance that a married couple desired a baby, but had not been able to conceive. I stated to the congregation what I heard The LORD say. I inquired if the couple or spouse was present. No one came forth. I was urged to ask if anyone in the congregation knew of a couple who had complications conceiving.

A well-known female in that church and community advised of a friend who is a pastor. He and his wife were unable to conceive due to complications. I requested that she "stand in the gap" for them. The congregation, her and I touched and agreed through prayer for their turnaround.

> *Therefore, I say to you, whatever things you ask when you pray, believe that you receive them, and you will have them.*
> *- Mark 11:24*

The LORD did just what we requested of Him.

Today, they are the proud parents of two beautiful and healthy children.

Book - Prophecies

Surely the Lord God does nothing, unless He reveals His secret to His servants the prophets.
- Amos 3:7
But he who prophesies speaks edification and exhortation and comfort to men.
- 1 Corinthians 14:3

"God said He is giving you until July to be finished writing the book."
- Apostle Otis Young Kingdom Life Tabernacle
2018

"April 2018, I hear the Spirit of The LORD whisper in my ear saying, this is the year of change, a time that brings freedom from problems as well as opportunities to improve your life...A year of change, freedom and unpredictability. Sales, advertising, writing, interviews, meetings, seminars, lectures, debates, and conferences will keep you busy..."
- Bishop Charlie Berrian
January 2018

"...There is revelation that God will give unto you. Your book will not be like no one else's book."
- Apostle Dr. LE Cohen, III
February 7, 2017

"God said it's time for you to get the book and the CD out!"

                - Bishop-Designate Dr. Kendric J. McMiller
                                         January 2016

"Lord, bless these writing fingers. You get that book out. It's going to be scary what God's going to do. It will be scary because God's putting you in fulltime ministry, because of the doors He's going to open for you! You do it just like He told you to; you have books in you."

                                    - Prophet Williams
                                          April 2014

"God is giving you until January to complete the book. It might not be published, but you will have finished writing it. It will not be what you think! It will open doors for you to go preach in big doors; preach at prophetic conferences. I see you being brought in to a church with a name something like "Shield of Faith." This will open the door for other preaching engagements. Places you will go, I won't even go preach. Through your pain and experiences, it is going to help other women. You will do it fulltime; don't worry about how. It is going to bless you. You will travel and be really busy: Chicago, Texas, Norway, and California."

                            - Apostle Dr. L.E. Cohen, III
                                        October 2013

"Bless this woman of God. May her album sell off the shelf, fly off the shelf in the name of Jesus! But The LORD said that the one you just did was not the one that He chose to do what He's about to do. IT's the project that's in your spirit that is going to be the one, because The LORD said that there was not just music in you, but there was also a book that is getting ready to come forth. And, the book, in reality, is what is going to cause the folk to look even the more at your music. Amen."

- Apostle LeAndrew Tyson
June 10, 2007

"There's money all around you; real estate. I see you doing bookkeeping, writing on journals, keeping notes. There's a book coming, it's some sort of motivational book, and know that it is God. Not too many Christians will receive it, but the secular world will."   - Prophetess Connie Williams
July 31, 2005

"I see you in Pensacola. I see you at the civic center and in auditoriums. I see a globe spinning, and you're going to Germany! God's opening doors. I see you traveling all over the world. I see gold; make sure you do something with gold."

- Dr. Vernette Rosier
April 28, 2005

About the Author

In the existence of every human resides a fame that is the epitome of their name. Angie means, "Heavenly Messenger."

This heavenly messenger was called in 1994 to preach the Gospel of Jesus Christ; is an ordained Elder and Prophetess; and, the Founder of Wellspring of Life International Ministries, an outreach ministry based in Tallahassee, FL. Angie ministers periodically to the female inmates of Gadsden Correctional Facility.

She was heard teaching and prophesying for eight years on the radio broadcast of 93.3FM in Quincy, FL, and Heaven 1410AM and 98.3FM in Tallahassee, FL. She was co-host on the In His Presence Cathedral of Praise Broadcast with her former pastor, Dr. L.E. Cohen, III.

She has a son, Brandon J. Wiggins, and has assisted executive administrators for more than 28 years. She is a graduate of Jefferson County Schools in Monticello, FL; and studied at Florida A&M University, Tallahassee Community College, and Lively Vo-Tech.

She is the business owner of Abundant Living Artwork, and author of the *When All Heaven Breaks Loose!* Newsletter that she wrote, published, marketed and distributed worldwide for seven years.

Angie loves yielding as The LORD's mouthpiece and servant, "for the perfecting of the saints, work of the ministry, and edifying of the body of Christ."

Order your copy

Spinderella

He Turned IT
Revised Edition

at:

ALK Coaching & Productions
Coaching@alkcopro.com

& Online Bookstores

www.ingramcontent.com/pod-product-compliance
Lightning Source LLC
Chambersburg PA
CBHW031423290426
44110CB00011B/504